THE POWER DELUSION

ANTHONY CAMPOLO, JR.

While this book is designed for the reader's personal enjoyment, it is also intended for group study. A Leader's Guide with Victor Multiuse Transparency Masters is available from your local bookstore or from the publisher.

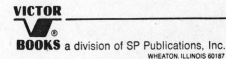

VICTOR

BOOKS a division of SP Publications, Inc.
WHEATON. ILLINOIS 60187

Offices also in
Whitby, Ontario, Canada
Amersham-on-the-Hill, Bucks, England

Recommended Dewey Decimal Classification: 261
Suggested Heading: POWER

Library of Congress Catalog Card Number: 83-061157
ISBN: 0-88207-292-7

© 1983 by SP Publications, Inc. All rights reserved
Printed in the United States of America

VICTOR BOOKS
A division of SP Publications, Inc.
    Wheaton, Illinois 60187

Contents

1 Power Plays in the Peaceable Kingdom
— Power Games for Christians   9

2 The Religious Macho Man
— A Mistaken View of Masculinity   17

3 The Hand That Cradles the Rock
— Women with Power   24

4 Chaos in Kiddie City
— When Children Get Power   32

5 Holy Terrors
— When the Clergy Forget Who They Are   42

6 Sanctified Power
— With a Church Like This, Who Needs Satan?   53

7 Glorious Authority
— The Way the Kingdom Comes   63

8 The Terrible Cost of Conquering Love
— Why God Withholds His Power   82

9 When All Else Fails
— What Happens When Power Must Be Used   97

10 The Need for Good People in a Bad World
— What Christians Should Do About Politics   108

11 What to Do While We Wait for the Second Coming
— A Christian Perspective on Civil
    Disobedience and Nuclear Disarmament   119

12 Resentment
— The Sin of the Powerless   136

13 Living Without Power
— The Triumph of Love   150

Foreword

I have long been convinced that one of the central manifestations of sin in 20th-century people is our neurotic need for control. We feverishly seek to manipulate, to be in charge. Yet, for all of the controlling we attempt, we can never seem to control what matters most: our relationship to God, our marriage, our children's destiny, our career. The irony is that the more we clamor to be in charge, the more we squeeze the life out of everything that is precious to us. Our longings for significance and security are God-given, but how we seek to meet these needs often is not. Ignoring Jesus' mandate that He be glorified in our weaknesses, we try to glorify God in the worldliness of our strengths, by being in control. Sometimes God must allow us to be wounded before we can learn relinquishment.

Anthony Campolo's book is about the freedom of relinquishment—the welcome relief of not having to be God, of submitting gladly our resignation as self-appointed managers of our own universe. Then we can learn the joy of the other side of control, the awesome beauty of the weakness of love. To this end Campolo deals perceptively with the perils of power, the chief enemy to love. Most of us are conscious of the abuse of power on the political level. We are less sensitive to the abuse of power in our interpersonal relationships—where it can be just as violent, just as manipulative, just as macho, and just as unChristlike, as when it occurs among nations. The fatal flaw of force, argues Campolo, is that it can never conquer the heart. Force can never conquer the power to love; only those who choose to be powerless servants of Christ can do that. In the end, *The Power Delusion* is a love story, a deeply moving invitation to empty ourselves of the need for control, of all the abuses of power, and to begin traveling light as Christ's agents of love through whom He will transform the world.

I have spoken at nearly a dozen conferences with Tony Campolo, and as a friend of mine once said, "You don't meet Tony Campolo, you *experience* him!"

Thus it would be tempting to regale the reader with stories. For I admire what everyone else does: his tremendous energy, his hilarity, the perceptiveness of his mind, the wideness of his heart, and an ability to communicate that few can surpass. But what touches me most is that his life demonstrates his message. People often ask me if I encounter much male chauvinism as a woman speaker. I am always grateful to acknowledge how little I have experienced. But at one conference the attitude toward women was appalling. It may have been unintentional. Yet I had never seen women treated, nor had I ever felt, so ignored, so second-class, or more like a nonentity. But it wasn't another woman who saw the sinfulness and injustice of the situation. It was Tony. He not only provided me with understanding, but he did everything possible to right a wrong. It would be very easy for someone with the enormity of his gifts and the tremendous response he invariably receives to simply bask in the applause and be blind to the oppressed around him. But Tony saw, cared deeply, and he did something about it. His life is what this book is all about.

Rebecca Manley Pippert
Washington D.C.
April 1983

To
Anne and Don Gray
for all their loving support

1
Power Plays in the Peaceable Kingdom

Power Games for Christians

Most people play power games.

There are husbands who want power over their wives and wives who try to gain equal power with their husbands. There are children who struggle to free themselves from the control of their parents and parents who tyrannize their children.

There are pastors who try to dominate their parishoners, and church members who want to control the clergy. There are employers who enjoy bossing their employees and employees who form unions so that they can dictate policies to employers.

There are white people who fear losing power over blacks and black people who turn cries of Freedom Now into shouts for Black Power. There are politicians who would compromise anything to stay in power and challengers who would use any deception to wrest power from the incumbents.

There are nations that willingly threaten human existence by building war machines which make them into world powers. There are world leaders who would push the button for an all-out nuclear war if their power were ever threatened.

Human beings hunger for power. German philosopher

Friedrich Nietzsche argued that this hunger is the essence of our humanity, that "the will to power" is the basic human drive. Sigmund Freud claimed that all our behavior can be explained as an attempt to satisfy sexual appetites. (In this, Freud is not far removed from what Paul says in Galatians 5:19–21.) Erich Fromm said that the desire to escape loneliness and separateness can explain our actions.

Nietzsche claimed that more basic than all other human needs is the craving to control one's own destiny, to be free to realize one's full potential without restraints from anyone. To be free from all limitations, to transcend the proscriptions of society and God, and to shrug off responsibility for others if such responsibility interferes with personal goals is, according to Nietsche, what every person naturally craves. He rejected any notion of a God, because he could not tolerate the thought of anyone more powerful than himself. He said that if there were gods, we would have to slay them out of jealousy.

While I am diametrically opposed to Nietzsche's atheistic beliefs, I appreciate his honest appraisal of things. Many social scientists, myself included, believe that his understanding of human nature is much more profound and far-reaching than that provided by Freud or by any other twentieth century writers. Strangely, what this enemy of Christianity says about human nature is very much in harmony with what the Bible teaches. Consequently, I lean heavily on his ideas as I develop my views on power.

Nietzsche clearly saw the hunger for power as anti-Christian. Consequently, he declared that Christianity should be abolished because it asks people to surrender to God, to render themselves as weak vessels to the Lord, and to reject attempts to exercise power over others. Nietzsche understood more clearly than most Christians that there is something about craving power which cannot be reconciled with the Christian lifestyle. He knew that Christ's call to servanthood and humility precludes all power games, and that Christ asks us to live contrary to our true nature. In short, to be coercive and Christian at the same time is impossible.

Christianity is a religion for people who acknowledge their weakness and want to make love the foundation of their lives. Because of this, Nietzsche rejected Christians as people who belong to the "herd" of inferior creatures. As he read the story of Cain and Abel, he declared Cain to be the superior of the two. He gladly acknowledged the fact that he bore the mark of Cain, who would not tolerate anyone to surpass him or receive greater glory.

This book is about power and about the things people do to get it. Power corrupts them and ultimately destroys them. This book is an attempt to show how a craving for power interferes with love and destroys personal relationships. The desire to be powerful interferes with the possibility of our being real Christians. This book is also an attempt to demonstrate that salvation lies in being surrendered to God, serving others, and giving up all attempts to be powerful.

Power and Authority

Before I go any further, it is important that I specify how I will be using the word *power*. I am defining power as "the prerogative to determine what happens and the coercive force to make others yield to your wishes—*even against their own will*." This last phrase is crucial, for the coercive nature of power gives expression to its potential for evil. Coercion is the crux of why power is irreconcilable with Christianity.

When a leader is able to persuade others to do his will without coercion, when he presents himself in such a way that people *want* to obey him, when they recognize him as a legitimate leader with the right to expect compliance with his wishes, I say that he has *authority*.

These definitions of power and authority are taken from the

writings of one of the greatest sociologists of all time, Max Weber. Since his day, most sociologists have employed definitions of power and authority that approximate these. Furthermore, most sociologists acknowledge a very significant relationship between power and authority. They notice that as power increases, authority decreases, and vice versa.

This relationship can readily be seen in the realm of government. A dictator can rule a nation with an iron hand and, by use of power, force people to do his will. He can suppress opposition and coerce people to comply with his wishes. However, the ruler who must rely on coercion lacks authority. His subjects do not love him nor do they recognize him as a legitimate ruler. If they have a chance, they will overthrow his regime; they do not consider it right that he should rule them. Examples of this condition abound in the world today. Afghanistan, Cambodia, and Uganda offer vivid illustrations of power at work.

On the other hand, there are governments which do not have to resort to power to force compliance with their rules and expectations. For the most part, their citizens want to cooperate with the government, believing that their elected officials have the right to rule. Such governments rule by authority.

Authority in the Family
What is true about power and authority in government is also true in other areas of life. For instance, in some families children are ruled by power. They are forced to obey their parents, to go to church and attend school. Parents function as dictators whose only way of getting their children to obey them is through threats of violent punishment for disobedience. The children do what they are told until they are old enough to resist their parents' will; then they rebel. The parents complain that they have lost "control" of their children. One father said he was afraid to tell his son what to do because the son was bigger than he was and would not hesitate to punch him out if he got too

demanding. Parents who have never established their authority in the home discover too late that they cannot exercise power over their children indefinitely.

Some parents establish relationships with their children that result in willing obedience to their wishes. The children realize that their parents want what is best for them. They know their parents are not self-interested as they make requests. They are pleased to show their love for their parents by yielding to their desires. Such parents, through sacrificial love, have brought their children into a love relationship in which they want to obey. Also, many of them have taught their children that the Bible has designated parents as persons to be obeyed and, hence, as legitimate rulers of the household. The children do not always like what is asked of them, nor do they always happily obey. But they still obey—not because they are forced to, but because deep down they want to. They know that obedience is right. Even as they grumble, they believe that their parents love them.

I am not suggesting that if a child is properly loved and instructed in Scripture he will automatically become a submissive child. What I am saying is that whatever the reason, when a parent must resort to force—and there are times when the best of parents must—there has been a decline in authority.

It is interesting to note that Jesus spoke with authority (Matthew 7:29). This distinguished Him from most of the Pharisees who could not elicit such respect. The disciples who gave their lives to Jesus did so willingly. Jesus forced no one to follow Him. He still earns people's allegiance through His sacrificial love, particularly as it was expressed on the cross. Speaking of His imminent crucifixion, He said, "I, if I be lifted up from the earth, will draw all men to Myself" (John 12:32, NASB). His love is sufficient; He will not force compliance with His will. He rules with authority and desires subjects who want to obey Him.

Will to Power

Contrary to Jesus, who willingly set aside His divine power when He came into the world to express His love, is Satan. The evil one lusted for power and that was what brought about his fall. The fact that God the Father had power greater than his was intolerable and this led him to seek ways to usurp the position of the heavenly King.

The great English poet, John Milton, rightly understood the motivations that lay behind Satan's rebellion against God. In his great epic poem, *Paradise Lost,* he has Satan say:

> To reign is worth ambition though in hell.
> Better to reign in hell, than serve in heaven.

Satan could not tolerate being less than all-powerful and it was this that necessitated his being thrown out of heaven.

Adam and Eve were tempted by Satan and it was their desire for power that allowed them to be seduced into sin. Satan told them that if they ate the forbidden fruit in the Garden of Eden, they would be like gods (Genesis 3). The original couple found this possibility too enticing to resist. Thus, original sin was born out of jealousy for God's power. It was the "will to power" that brought the curse of sin and suffering upon the human race.

Love

We should not conclude from all this that power is inherently evil. We must remember that God has power and God is good. However, the primary use of power is to destroy and restrain. With power God destroys the work of Satan. With power He destroys the corruptive works of the human race. God employs His power to hold back the forces of evil. He ordains governments to restrain the evil inherent in society. His power can destroy diseases. He can annihilate viruses and cancers. In the end He will destroy all powers that will not surrender. No one who reads the Psalms can be unaware of the power of God. With His power, He will put down the enemies of the righteous and with His power He will bring to nothing the prideful works of people.

This book, however, emphasizes that creative tendency in God which is expressed in His love. His love creates, heals, and saves. Tielhard de Chardin, the French theologian and anthropologist, points out that love is whatever unifies or brings things together. Thus, it is with love that God creates the universe. Electrons are unified with protons to form atoms. Atoms of various kinds are unified to form molecules. Molecules are unified to form amino acids. And so the process continues.

God created all things and He did so through His love. It is love that brings things together. It is love that heals. Troubled hearts and minds are made whole through His love. The physical body is restored through love. Ultimately, the entire universe will be healed by love (Romans 8:18–22). In the end, He will unify the world under His rule (Ephesians 1:18–22).

In God's dealing with us, we experience both His love and His power. His love saves us and heals us. His love makes us into new creatures (2 Corinthians 5:17). On the other hand, His power destroys in us all that is corrupt and unclean. His power purges and leaves us pure. Power is coercive whereas love is entreating. And that is why I say that God saves us by His love. He does not force His way into our lives, nor does He coerce us into submission. Instead, He entreats us with His love. He presents Himself to us not in the awesome splendor of His power but in weakness on a cross. There He shows us love in the most perfect expression.

We are fools if we do not respond to so great a love. To reject His love is to invite His use of power, and with His power comes the destruction of what will not yield to His love. This is the beautiful and frightening character of reality.

The ruling style of Adam and his heirs is contrary to the

nature and behavior of Christ. What was the original sin, if not jealousy for God's power? What was it that caused the original couple to lose Eden, if not the desire to be like gods? What was the act that brought on the curse of that first transgression, if not the will to be powerful?

The first Adam sought power and set aside love. The second Adam, Christ, willingly set aside power (Philippians 2) and took the risks essential for love.

2
The Religious Macho Man

A Mistaken View of Masculinity

Willard Waller did most of his writing during the 1930s. For four decades his brilliant insights into family life were largely ignored, until recently when his work was rediscovered. What he has to say about dating and marriage is very relevant to our discussion of power.

Waller's own marriage, like the marriage of his parents, was a disaster. After years of bitterness and pain, he and his wife were divorced. As he studied the marriage of others, he became aware that many married people suffered profound unhappiness and stayed together only because of religious reasons or family obligations.

Amazed at how many unhappy marriages he came across in his studies, Waller tried to discover the cause of all of this misery and failure. He found his answer in the craving for power inherent in human nature.

In both dating and marriage, each person endeavors to gain power over his or her partner. One way to do this is to withhold love. Therefore, the person who loves the least has the most power, and the person who loves the most has the least power. Waller calls this "the principle of least interest."

Loving Less

All of us have seen this principle expressed in real-life situations. In serious dating, the person who is least in love, and least interested in continuing the relationship, is in control and can call the shots. Think of some high school girl who is desperately in love. Her boyfriend, on the other hand, has only limited interest in her. In such a situation, he has great power over her and can make her do whatever he wants. She obeys his wishes because she is afraid of losing him. She may even submit to sexual relations with him, in spite of the fact that premarital sex is contrary to her religious convictions. Because she loves him so much, and he loves her so little, she is powerless. Because she desperately wants to continue the relationship, at all costs, she is vulnerable to his every whim.

Without ever learning Waller's "principle of least interest," most young people instinctively understand how it works. In dating, each partner is cautious about loving too much for fear of the consequences. Each tries to get the other person to love the most, and neither dares to love until he or she is sure that the other person is at least equally in love.

A young man deliberately develops a line which is aimed at convincing the young woman that he loves her more than he really does. He tells her he has never felt this way with anyone before, has never experienced anything like this love surging through him, that he never knew it could be so wonderful, etc. If she buys the line, she may risk falling in love with him, and then he's got her where he wants her.

The girl, on the other hand, is probably not naive. She has learned the hard way not to believe everything she hears from a courting lad. She is all too well aware of the stakes in this game and knows what she stands to lose. With caution, she parries the line and prides herself on her ability not to be taken in. She does her best to get him to *really* be in love without allowing herself to become too emotionally involved.

And so the game is played, each person trying to love *less,* each withholding love to gain power over the other, each afraid to love because it would mean a loss of power.

When the game is laid out this clearly, its horrible character is exposed. What God means to be a mutually gratifying relationship is perverted into a destructive power struggle. Instead of following God's design to love each other, people withhold love because of their desire for power.

Don Juan and Carmen

One of the ugly consequences of preferring power to love is what can be called the Don Juan Syndrome. The young man feels great satisfaction in persuading a long succession of females to fall head over heels in love with him while he remains emotionally detached. He takes pride in his ability to bring women under his control while keeping himself free from involvement. He sees each woman who falls for him as a conquest. But like the classical Don Juan, he never experiences the gratification that comes from love.

He is afraid of love because he knows that loving will make him vulnerable to the callous treatment he has given to others. He is never satisfied with his conquests because power always leaves the conqueror hungry for more conquests and power. And he has established a style of relating to women that will never allow him the fulfillment of love. His shallow victories leave him empty; in gratifying his desire to bring women under his control, he has lost the capacity to love.

Men are not the only ones guilty of viewing members of the opposite sex as things to be conquered rather than persons to be loved. There are women who play the game. Women who seek to bring men under their control without really loving them are suffering from what I call the Carmen Syndrome. Such a woman plays with men's emotions and, like Carmen in Verdi's opera, mocks their cravings to possess her. She flirts and entices, and then laughs at the men who are seduced by her wiles. She too ends up victimized by her own cruelty, as she loses the capacity to love.

James Bond

When Elvis Presley sang his pleading song, "Don't Be Cruel to a Heart That's True," he gave expression to what so many young people have experienced in their love lives. In loving they become vulnerable to the abuse of a partner who exploits with the power that comes from loving less.

The James Bond movies pick up the same theme. Bond, better known as Agent 007 of the British Secret Service, is able to get women to fall in love with him while he remains cool and detached. Because he gains power over them in this manner, he can persuade these women to provide sexual pleasure and also to help him in his spying activities, even if, in the process, the women must betray former loyalties. Unfortunately, James Bond has become a model for too many men in the Western world. Being "cool" or emotionally detached has become a trait to imitate. The problem with the James Bonds of the world is that they play it cool so long that they lose the capacity to ever be passionate. Passion requires that the individual surrender to the desires of his or her partner. This the followers of James Bond would never do, because they are deluded into thinking that it is better to hold power than to be passionately in love.

Love Versus Power

Being afraid to express love begins early in life. I remember telling one of my eighth grade friends that I really liked a particular girl. It was about the worst thing I could have done. My friend threatened to tell her and I almost died. I told him I would do anything he wanted, as long as he kept secret how much I liked that girl.

My "friend" got a lot of mileage out of that offer. What was I afraid of, anyway? What was it that so horrified me? That's simple. I was afraid she would know that I liked her without my knowing if she liked me. And if she didn't like me, I would have been so vulnerable. She might have laughed at me and I would have been powerless to prevent my humiliation. I would rather she never knew I liked her than to be vulnerable to humiliation. She never did know how I felt. This is the price of being in control and remaining invulnerable.

The game continues in high school. Milton Friedenburg tells us in his excellent book on teenage life, *Coming of Age in America,* that high school status is determined by how many persons of the opposite sex a teenager can get to fall in love with him or her. Popularity in high school is dependent on nothing more than "turning on" members of the opposite sex, but without falling for any of them. In the subculture of high school life, young people are being conditioned to prefer power to love.

What is true of dating carries over into marriage, according to Willard Waller. Men particularly have been deluded by the temptation to be powerful, and they end up wanting to dominate their wives. Sometimes they are led to think that a Christian husband is merely a spiritualized version of Macho Man. They have heard too many misguided sermons from preachers who proclaim that God designed women to want to be dominated. As they have tried to bring their wives under their control, these men have deliberately restrained their own tendency to love. I am amazed at how many women have complained to me in counseling sessions that their husbands never tell them they love them. When I confronted one husband with his wife's complaint, he said, "Twenty-eight years ago when I married her, I told her I loved her and that if I ever changed my mind, I would let her know."

Men recognize that in loving their wives they lose their

power to dominate. And yet, that is exactly what the Bible teaches them to do. To love one's wife is to live in a vulnerable condition wherein one can be hurt. Furthermore, the man who loves does not always seek to have his own way, because love does not behave this way (1 Corinthians 13:5).

Too many men view the consequences of loving as counter to their view of being manly. They would rather be "real men" than to love. Satan deludes them with the will to power. As they follow the delusion, they lose the capacity for the greatest of human joys, the thrill of loving.

The craving for power is so important to some men that it ruins their ability to enjoy a normal sex life. The sexual act ceases to be a means for expressing love and becomes an exercise in demonstrating power. Every marriage counselor can tell of cases wherein the husband fails to be aroused unless he can reduce his wife to servile and humiliating behavior. His aphrodisiac is power. Love does not stimulate him at all.

You may question whether this point need be made. To this I can resoundingly answer yes! Too many Christian women have too often and too long had to endure degradation at the hands of their husbands, to allow such practices to continue unchallenged. Just because a couple is legally married, with benefit of clergy, does not give a husband the right to turn their sexual relations into expressions of domination. Too many "Christian" men have taken the verse, "Wives, submit yourselves unto your husbands," to mean that wives should submit to indignities which make the men dizzy with a perverted sense of power.

Rape, say psychologists, should not even be considered a sexual act. It is an exercise of power. There can be no greater power exercised by one human being over another than the ability to humiliate the other person without that one having recourse or means of refusal. There is a lot of rape going on in so-called Christian marriages. Nobody dares talk about it.

Well, I am talking about it now and saying as clearly as I know how that God condemns such behavior. Those who believe that women are ordered by God to submit to such dehumanization are blasphemers.

3
The Hand That Cradles the Rock

Women with Power

Women also play power games. And because our society considers it improper for them to be aggressive, they play with great subtlety. Often it is through their attractiveness that they are able to exercise power over men. Many women realize that they can control men through sex. Undoubtedly, many a man has been manipulated down the aisle because it was the only way he could enjoy the pleasures of sexual relations. Mothers, especially of a generation ago, taught their daughters to use sex in such a manner. The daughters were warned, "If you give yourself to him without his marrying you, he never will. After all, why should he marry when he can get what he wants without marrying?" Statements like this set forth a low view of marriage and of males, teaching the girls that sex was something to be used to get men to do what females wanted.

Women who withhold sex from their husbands in order to gain power can be victimized by their own schemes. Such women often become sexually frigid because they are afraid to let themselves go with their husbands. They have been conditioned to associate the withholding of sex with power, and they are afraid to be passionate with their spouses.

24

Sadly, some of these women overcome their sexual inhibitions through infidelity. When having sex on a one-night stand with a partner they will never see again, they can experience the sexual release they are incapable of with their marital partners. Once again we have evidence that the desire to have power corrupts relationships and destroys love.

For the most part, I did not join the chorus of critics who attacked Marabel Morgan's controversial book, *The Total Woman.* Some people with a liberal, secular bias thought Morgan's words supported a role for women that denied them their self-actualization and dignity. However, most of us in the evangelical community realized that the book was aimed at church women who had been reared to view sex as a "wifely duty" rather than something to be enjoyed. To these women, Morgan's book was a liberating manifesto that freed them for improved relations with their mates.

I do, however, have one major objection to the book. I think that Morgan encourages women to use sex in a manipulative fashion. She suggests that women should abandon nagging as a means of getting what they want from their husbands and should resort to being sexually seductive. Morgan proposes that women make their husbands receptive to their requests by gratifying their sexual desires.

While there may be some positive aspects to this suggestion, I object to sex being used to manipulate husbands. I think God means sex as an expression of married love. When it is a means to gain control of a husband, it is perverted. There can be many unintended and negative consequences to such a strategy, including the husband's feeling of "being had."

Women's Lib
The female play for power is nowhere more evident than in the women's liberation movement. Many of the claims of the women's libbers have great validity for the Christian as well as for the

secular person. Both Jesus and the Apostle Paul initiated ideas that allow women to view themselves as equal with men, possessing identity of their own, and having the right to express the potential inherent in their gifts and abilities.

Nevertheless, there are dangers in the women's movement that are only now being recognized by some of its most ardent supporters. There is no question that women had the right to condemn what had been done to them by 35 million aggressive, domineering, pushy husbands. However, the answer to 35 million aggressive, domineering, pushy husbands is not to create an opposition of 35 million aggressive, domineering, pushy wives. If the only answer to husbands who push their wives around is to teach wives to push back, we are in a war between the sexes.

Fortunately, the Bible has a healing solution to the growing tension between mates sparked by women's efforts to affirm their dignity. From a biblical point of view, there is nothing wrong with a woman being submissive to her husband. That is exactly what the Bible teaches (Ephesians 5:22). To abandon power plays and to render herself vulnerable to her husband is a precondition for love.

However, the Bible also asks husbands to be submissive. Before any chauvinist distorts Ephesians 5:22, he should read the verse immediately preceding which instructs husbands and wives to submit themselves to each other. In Ephesians 5:25, husbands are told, "Love your wives, just as Christ loved the church and gave Himself up for her." Christ loved the church by becoming her servant and by sacrificing Himself to the uttermost in order that the church, His bride (Revelation 21:2, 9) might have her every need met and be made complete in every way.

If you want to know how the servant role was carried out in those days, read how Jesus got down on His knees to wash His disciples' feet (John 13:3–10). When Peter objected to this action on the part of the Lord, Jesus made it clear that those who failed to understand why He washed their feet could not be part of His kingdom. In the kingdom of God, love is expressed in servanthood; husbands who seek to love their wives as Christ loved the church find they have much to learn.

One day, while hosting my early morning TV talk show, I had a guest who had authored a book that was destined to become "must" reading for feminists. During the interview I questioned her thesis that wives should live somewhat independently of their husbands. She responded by asking, "You're not suggesting that I should sacrifice my personal fulfillment and career aspirations and self-actualization for my husband and children, are you?"

I replied emphatically, "Yes! There's nothing wrong with a woman sacrificing her personal aspirations, career goals, or her program for self-actualization to serve her husband and children. That's what marriage is all about. Nobody said you had to make those sacrifices—you could have stayed single. But since you got married, you should put the well-being of your family above yourself. If you have a good marriage, your husband will make the same kind of commitment. He will put what happens to you and the children above the realization of his own personal goals and will consider the self-actualization of each family member more important than anything that happens to him."

There were letters from the TV audience, criticizing my response. But the more I think about it, the more I support what I said that day. A good marriage is one in which each considers the other better than himself or herself (Philippians 2:3). When a wife puts her husband's well-being above her own, she is doing the right and biblical thing. Unfortunately, too many husbands fail to reciprocate in like manner.

I know of one husband who was given the opportunity for a major promotion with his employer, General Electric. The company offered him a high executive position which would have required a move from suburban Philadelphia to Schenectady, New York. He took the job immediately when it was offered, without talking things over with his wife and children. He came home from work that evening, bounding into the house with news he thought would be greeted with joy. Instead, the word of his promotion created sadness and consternation. He had assumed that since the promotion was what he wanted, his wife and children would be thrilled too.

He failed to consider what the move would mean to anybody else. He gave no thought to the fact that his wife would have to leave a fulfilling job and many close friends. He had no feeling for the sadness of his children who would have to leave a high school they loved. This man's daughter was a swimming star on the school team and his son was president of the junior class. Both were supposed to walk away from such things without a thought, simply because Daddy had a chance to get something he wanted. In a typically phony manner, the frustrated father declared, "I'm only doing it for the family!" His wife and children could have responded, "Who are you kidding?"

One way to handle such a situation would be for the man to bring home the news of the offered promotion and then tell his family that he probably wouldn't take it because it would interfere with opportunities that made them happy. He would put his wife's goals and the happiness of his children above his own self-interest. On the other hand, his wife and children could respond to the announcement by telling him that they would gladly make whatever sacrifice necessary so that he could have what was best for him. In doing so, they would all be fulfilling the biblical admonition to prefer one another in love.

If love was expressed, rather than a desire for power, they would have no problem, because love never seeks to have its own way. "It is not rude, it is not self-seeking, it is not easily angered, it keeps no record of wrongs" (1 Corinthians 13:5).

Ideally, the Christian family is democratic in nature. All the members see themselves as equals before God. This does not necessarily do away with the role of leadership of the father. For in a democracy there is always a leader. However, in a democracy the leader does not see himself as an autocrat, but rather deems himself an equal to those he leads. His leadership is never tyrannical. He does not force his will on others, but instead expresses the will of his people.

The Bible teaches that wherever two or three are gathered together in Christ's name, He will be in their midst (Matthew 18:20). That means that when family members together seek the leading of the Lord, He will make His will known to them. A family should pray and discuss the issues until they are of one accord. When this has been done, the unanimous opinion should be taken to be the Lord's will. God makes His will known to any body of believers who prayerfully seek His will and wait until His Spirit creates unanimity.

The ideal Christian family is made up of individuals who are ready to surrender their own advantage for the good of others. Members of such a family prayerfully seek what God would have them do rather than pursuing fulfillment of personal ambitions.

Unfortunately, the ideal is seldom found. Too often, men seek their own way without regard for other family members. This kind of behavior inevitably leads to rebellion. It is against such familial tyranny that many Christian women shout their protests and call for liberation. They are tired of being submissive to men who do not know how to love them as Christ loved the church.

Who's in Charge?

Every once in a while, when I am conducting a family life program in some church, a man stands during the question-and-answer time and says, "You haven't answered the most important question: Who's supposed to be the head of the house?"

To that I quickly respond, "If you understood Jesus, you wouldn't ask such a question. That's the same kind of question the mother of James and John asked."

Then the mother of Zebedee's sons came to Jesus with her sons and, kneeling down, asked a favor of Him.
"What is it you want?" He asked.
She said, "Grant that one of these two sons of mine may sit at Your right and the other at Your left in Your kingdom."
"You don't know what you are asking," Jesus said to them. "Can you drink the cup I am going to drink?"
"We can," they answered.
Jesus said to them, "You will indeed drink from My cup, but to sit at My right or left is not for Me to grant. These places belong to those for whom they have been prepared by My Father."
When the ten heard about this, they were indignant with the two brothers. Jesus called them together and said, "You know that the rulers of the Gentiles lord it over them, and their high officials exercise authority over them. Not so with you. Instead, whoever wants to become great among you must be your servant, and whoever wants to be first must be your slave—just as the Son of Man did not come to be served, but to serve, and to give His life as a ransom for many" (Matthew 20:20–28).

Jesus made it clear that His kingdom had no place for power-seekers, for His was a kingdom of servants. The Christian never asks, "How can I be master?" Instead, he asks, "How can I be servant?" The Christian never asks, "How can I be number one?" Instead he asks, "How can I be the last and the least?"

No one should be ashamed of assuming a servant role. Too many times women are made to feel that they should apologize for being mothers and housewives. In reality, such roles can be noble callings. When I was on the faculty of the University of Pennsylvania, there were gatherings from time to time to which faculty members brought their spouses. Inevitably, some woman lawyer or sociologist would confront my wife with the question, "And what is it that you do, my dear?" My wife, who is one of the most brilliantly articulate individuals I know, had a great response: "I am socializing two homo sapiens into the dominant values of the Judeo-Christian tradition in order that they might be instruments for the transformation of the social order into the telelogically prescribed utopia inherent in the eschaton."

When she followed that with, "And what is it that you do?" the other person's, "A lawyer," just wasn't that overpowering.

It is no wonder Christ's Gospel is misunderstood. He glorifies powerlessness in a world that worships power. He offers meekness to those who teach aggressiveness. His message is foolishness to those committed to a lifestyle that prefers power to love. What is sad is that the most flagrant failure to understand the call of Christ to relinquish power, to discover strength in weakness, and to prefer meekness and love to domination and control, should occur within the body of people who claim to be His followers.

Jesus leaves little room in His kingdom for male chauvinists who distort Scripture in order to legitimate their oppression of women. His Gospel is in opposition to any women's movement that seeks to put down men, while calling upon the sisterhood to be powerful. His kingdom requires mutual submission.

Servanthood is not servility. Rather, it is the means through which we each realize our own potential.

4
Chaos in Kiddie City

When Children Get Power

Power struggles in the family are not confined to husbands and wives. Increasingly, children have gotten into the action, and many parents find their offspring very difficult to control.

In the agrarian society when most people were farmers, the husband was generally head of the household. However, in this century, America has become an urban industrial society. This transition has greatly diminished the autocratic control that so many men had over their families. When they were farmers, men worked and lived at the same place. Children worked with their fathers and the fathers supervised their activities. When farming was no longer the dominant vocation for Americans and men left their homes to work in the office or factory, they lost contact and control at home.

In the absence of Father, it would seem natural for Mother to take over control of the children. But in most American homes, mothers have proven themselves incapable of assuming control. They have been victimized by what I choose to call the Cult of Momism.

From a host of sources, mothers have been told that their

primary function is to be love machines. Freud in psychology and John Dewey in educational studies both taught that the mother's love is a determining factor in the early socialization of children. Magazines like *Redbook, Women's Day,* and *Ladies' Home Journal* have carried countless articles popularizing this view. Television talk shows from the "Tonight" show to Phil Donahue's program have communicated this principle so widely that it has become a cultural truism. Constantly, mothers have gotten the message that their children are supposed to love them intensely and at all times. It is difficult for a woman to exercise control when she desires above all to be loved. Most mothers are afraid of incurring the resentment of their children by disciplining them.

The result of all this is obvious. If fathers do not control the family because they are absent from morning till night, and mothers are afraid to control their children because they fear incurring resentment, the children can end up dominating their families. For the first time in history, the filiocentric or child-centered family has become normative. Children seem to rule most families.

If there is any question as to what I am talking about, go to a supermarket and watch the interaction between young children and their mothers. Time and time again, you will see the mothers giving in to their children's demands. The children seem to be able to get almost anything they want simply by threatening temper tantrums. In short, children have assumed positions of power.

Insecure Parents

Another disturbing development in family relations has resulted from the growth of professionalism in rearing children. From the time that Harry Stack Sullivan provided his vision of the role of social scientists in producing properly socialized children, parents have been led to doubt their own ability to successfully raise their children. Sociologists, psychologists, and social workers have often left parents with the impression that the techniques essential to the rearing of children are possessed only by experts who have been specially trained for the task. They have argued that most parents do not know enough to parent effectively. Accordingly, these social scientists suggest that childrearing should be professionalized. This means either that children should be reared in nursery schools with trained personnel or that all mothers and fathers should be put through parenting courses to learn how to do the job right. All of this tends to call the authority of parents into question and even causes the parents to doubt themselves. Consequently, the leadership effectiveness of parents has eroded, and children have seized the opportunity to assert themselves.

Just for the record, it should be affirmed that parents know more about rearing children than many of the "experts" give them credit for. Most parents do a pretty decent job. On the other hand, social scientists are not nearly as effective as they would like us to believe. The Hans Eysenck study points out that of the emotionally disturbed people who go for psychoanalysis, 44 percent improve within a year. Of those who go for psychotherapy, 64 percent improve within a year, and of those who go for no treatment at all, 72 percent improve within a year.

I am not suggesting that counseling is useless. When it is based on biblical principles, it can be effective and produce wonderful results. I am simply illustrating why parents need not be threatened by the so-called expertise of social scientists. Loving Christian parents tend to do a good job of raising their children simply by trusting their instincts and following biblical teachings about childrearing.

Need for Norms
Still another cause for the decline of parental authority and the

increase of power for children can be found in the rapidly changing societal norms of today. Our world is changing so quickly that parents are confused about what they should expect from their children. When parents endeavor to direct the lives of their children by telling them what they cannot do, they are often challenged with, "But all the other kids are doing it." Insecure parents, afraid of forcing their children into a lifestyle that would be unacceptable to their peers, give in under such pressure, allowing the children to gain still more power.

It is quite easy to demonstrate the destructive results of possessing power, as we study the effect on children. Erik Erikson, one of the leading figures in the field of human development, noted that children become emotionally disturbed when they possess power they cannot responsibly handle. They become frustrated when they find themselves in control of their lives and in control of their parents. Children need restraints and enforced rules. If life does not have order to it, children go into depression.

Emile Durkheim, one of the pioneers in sociological research, discovered that without clearly defined norms and rules to govern life, people become self-destructive and even suicidal. Drug use, alcoholism, and delinquency are related to normlessness. In light of this fact, it is easy to see how lack of regulation in the lives of contemporary youth has been a major source of the destructive problems that emotionally cripple so many young people.

Defiance of parental authority has become a hallmark of our times. More and more parents complain about their inability to control their children. Many of them realize their children are more influenced by the crowd they run with than by the teachings of home and church. Parental efforts to enforce rules and regulations are often greeted with open defiance. This has created such hurt and dismay that a surprising number of parents admit that if they had it to do over again, they would not have any children.

When children exercise power, they often destroy the possibilities for love, and parents accept their leaving home with relief. The children may have little concern for the feeling of their parents, thinking they have gained something because they are now free to do what they want. However, such children are usually extremely unhappy and malcontented. They have gained power but have lost love. And they don't realize that what they've lost is much more important than what they've gained.

Tough Love

We all know families in which the children have gotten out of hand; yet most of us sense an inability to give much advice that is helpful. Some parents have resorted to a program called Tough Love, in which parents try to establish and enforce strict rules with a rebellious child. This tactic is often a plan of last resort, as parents endeavor to be brutally strict in the hope that the child will straighten out. The child is confronted with the threat of serious punishment if rules are not obeyed. The parents even threaten to throw the child out of the home if their wishes are violated. Sometimes this plan seems to work, but in many cases it does not. It is an all-or-nothing approach to the problem. The child either submits or else. This may result in the child leaving home for good. The parents are aware of this possibility when they enter into the program, but they are usually so desperate that they are willing to take the risk.

I know of one extreme case of family conflict which resulted in the children murdering their father. He resorted to the tactics of Tough Love and punished his two children after they openly defied him. He told them that they would be confined to the home for a week because of their disobedience. One evening he went out and his children decided that they would kill him when he got home. They lay in wait several hours and when he returned home, they ambushed him in the driveway and shot him. These children refused to have their power limited and killed their own father because he interfered with their desires.

Most problems with children do not approach such extremes. But even in ordinary families, children are usurping power in self-destructive ways. Everyone is aware that young people need more restraints and controls placed upon them. The young people themselves recognize that they have too much power for their own good. In a recent study of graduating high school seniors, a significant majority reported that they wished their parents had established better control over them as they were going through school. Most young people realize that parental regulations are usually good for them and are expressions of love.

Willful Children

It is quite simple to recognize the problem, but it is difficult to supply a solution. Even children who are not raised in a permissive manner may exert themselves against parental authority. Every once in a while, a child raised in the church becomes openly defiant to his parents' wishes and some church member offhandedly quips, "Train up a child in the way he should go and when he is old he will not depart from it." Usually the person who so readily quotes this verse from Proverbs does not have any children. Parents know that rearing children is just not that simple in the modern world.

A child's training comes from a multitude of sources in addition to his parents. The school, peers, neighbors and, above all, television and radio all communicate values of lifestyles to our young people. Often the messages from these outside sources are diametrically opposed to what the parents are trying to communicate. In comparison with these alternate agents of socialization, the parents often appear naive and out of date.

Children are not Pavlovian dogs who simply act as they are trained. We all know parents who have brought up their children "right" only to have them disastrously rebel. We also know of others who break every prescription for parenting and yet have model children. Children have wills of their own and can easily be tempted to seek the power to control their own lives without reference to anyone. Sometimes parents are able to break their wills; but in other cases, toughness on the part of parents only results in the children being more defiant.

The demonic lures children to seek power even if it means forfeiting love, and children are often seduced by the evil one. In our modern age people do not like to hear a sociologist talk about Satan. Nevertheless, this sociologist is convinced that there is an evil presence that tempts children as well as adults to seek power, regardless of the consequences.

When the child or teenager comes to recognize the Bible as an ultimate authority for his behavior, the problem is well on its way to being solved. If this is to be the case, however, the parents must let the child know in his earliest days that the Bible is the ultimate source of authority in their lives too. When a child realizes that his parents are not arbitrary rulers but are themselves obedient to a higher law, it encourages him to view Scripture as deserving of respect. Parents must make a child see that what they require is in accord with the teachings of Scripture. Instead of establishing rules by declaring, "Because I said so!" as is often the case, parents should be ready to show that what they ask is in accord with God's will and God's Word.

It is obvious that parents cannot come up with a verse for every situation in life. But they should try to explain the basic principles of right and wrong set forth in Scripture and show how the rules they are establishing are in accord with those principles. Obviously, this will require more Bible study on the part of parents than is now typically the case. Children need to know that there is a law higher than their parents on which the parents base their demands. Bright children constantly respond to orders set forth by their parents with the direction question, "Why?" They are seeking the reasons that lie behind the parental command. The answer, "Because I said so!" is not enough for most intelligent children. Parents must be able to relate their requests to the teachings of Scripture.

Sometimes the occasion does not permit a lengthy exposition of the biblical basis for what is being demanded. However, if children are made aware that their parents' commands are not based on arbitrary whims but rather on the teachings of an absolute authority, they will be willing to obey and wait for an explanation later. What is essential is that they know their parents are ruling in submission to the rule of God. Then they will perceive their parents as having authority and will be more likely to want to obey them.

While there may be many things to criticize about Bill Gothard's Basic Youth Conflict seminars, there is one thing that must be admitted—he makes clear that the authority of parents is based on the higher authority of God's Word. When the Bible says, "Children, obey your parents in the Lord" (Ephesians 6:1), it is making exactly this point. If parents accept the authority of Scripture and their children do too, then the children will be obedient to their parents. I know of many cases of children who had been incorrigible but became submissive to their parents after a conversion experience. To be Christian is to prefer love to power. The more children love their parents, the less they want the power to defy them.

Relinquishing Control

Parents also must learn lessons about power and its destructive influence on the way they relate to their children. Parents who enjoy having children under their control tend to encourage unhealthy dependency. By constantly doing for children what the children can do for themselves, such parents are able to maintain power over them.

At Eastern College where I teach, I observed a young woman who was kept under the domination of her parents throughout her college career. Her parents came to visit her every weekend and took home her dirty clothes to launder. They gave their daughter everything she might request. If she had problems in a course, her parents would call on the professor to discuss the problems. If she had difficulty with her roommate, they would complain to the dean of students. By constantly doing things for her, they prevented her from ever growing up. She remained dependent and under her parents' control. She never married and they still take care of her. These parents would claim that they love their daughter, but they do not love her enough to let her go. They so much enjoy having her under their control that they have destroyed the possibility for her independent happiness.

Parents must learn how to relinquish control over their children. Love requires it. It is painful for parents to watch their children do things which are self-defeating and hurtful, but loving parents endure this suffering rather than interfere with their children's growing right to be on their own. Loving parents know how to give up power as an expression of love.

Only parents who are not afraid of losing power are capable of having an honest relationship with their children. For instance, when a parent does something wrong and a child is the victim of that wrongdoing, the parent should ask the child for forgiveness. Unfortunately, many parents are reluctant to do this. They are anxious to preserve an image of infallibility and omnipotence with their children and fear that confessing their failures would hurt that image. Consequently, they maintain a facade of having done nothing wrong, even when this is not the case. Children learn from their parents; if the parents never admit when they have been wrong, then neither will the children. This may ultimately affect their ability to be Christians. Having been conditioned never to confess faults or ask for forgiveness, such children may find it impossible to confess their sins to God and ask for His forgiveness. Playing the power game can ultimately separate children from the love of God. Such is the price to be paid when we are afraid to give up power.

5
Holy Terrors

When the Clergy
Forget Who They Are

Few people know the rhetoric of servanthood better than the clergy. And yet so many of them, even unconsciously, are on power trips. It may be that some were attracted to the ministry because they saw in the role of minister the opportunity to exercise power. Clergymen of this type have learned to play their power games with a cleverness that keeps most people from ever suspecting what they are really about.

One way for the minister to gain and maintain power is to do all the work of the church himself. As a young pastor I was very guilty of this tactic. I called on all the church members, ran the youth groups and the Daily Vacation Bible School, supervised the Sunday School, mimeographed the church bulletin, organized the church choir, unofficially chaired every committee, and did half of the janitorial work. For the most part, the church people stood back in amazement at my boundless energy and seeming dedication. Yet what I was really doing was keeping church members out of positions of power by occupying them all myself. I was in charge of everything. I controlled the church and my power was everywhere evident. When church members wanted to take over some of the roles I monopolized, I treated them as threatening people. When I met with fellow clergy of my community, our discussions often revolved around ways to handle such uppity members.

"Don't they realize what I am trying to accomplish?" "Why do they want to hold me back?" "Why are they interfering with my plans?" "If they would just move out of my way, I could really get the church rolling!"

I am sure these thoughts are common to many young pastors just out of seminary. And I wonder how many of them give up on being pastors simply because they cannot have their own way or persuade the church members to comply with their dictates. I also wonder how many church members have been stymied in their Christian growth because they have not had opportunity to exercise their gifts within the body of Christ. Scripture teaches that God gives out gifts to all Christians and that each should be allowed to exercise his or her gift.

The body is a unit, though it is made up of many parts; and though all its parts are many, they form one body. So it is with Christ. For we were all baptized by one Spirit into one body— whether Jews or Greeks, slave or free—and we were all given the one Spirit to drink.

Now the body is not made up of one part but of many. If the foot should say, "Because I am not a hand, I do not belong to the body," it would not for that reason cease to be part of the body. And if the ear should say, "Because I am not an eye, I do not belong to the body," it would not for that reason cease to be part of the body. If the whole body were an eye, where would the sense of hearing be? If the whole body were an ear, where would the sense of smell be? But in fact God has arranged the parts in the body, every one of them, just as He wanted them to be (1 Corinthians 12:12–18).

Unfortunately, some clergymen do not apply this passage to

themselves. Rather, they act as if a minister is the whole body of Christ and leave room for no one else to do anything significant. Ideally, the pastor should recognize that his primary work is to enable church members to take over the various responsibilities essential to a healthy congregation. He should help them discover their gifts and abilities, and show how those talents can be used in the work of the church. He should train the members of his congregation to effectively minister, through their respective abilities, to the needs of the congregation and to the world outside the church. This is what Paul was suggesting in the Letter to the Ephesians:

> It was He who gave some to be apostles, some to be prophets, some to be evangelists, and some to be pastors and teachers, to prepare God's people for works of service, so that the body of Christ may be built up (4:11–12).

Pastors who try to do everything themselves often complain about the lack of adequate lay leadership in the church. In reality, they are keeping lay workers out of leadership roles because of their own need for power. Sometimes a power-oriented pastor will con his congregation into hiring an assistant pastor whom he can control; then the two of them are able to do all the church work, and it becomes unnecessary for the church members to do anything. The pastor is more powerful than ever, the church program grinds on, and the laity remain unchallenged and dormant.

I presently belong to a church of almost 3,000 members. The pastor has a brilliant capability to motivate members of the church to do many tasks that are often considered the prerogative of the professional clergy. The result is a dynamic congregation with responsible leadership and not a single paid assistant. My pastor finds it unnecessary to play power games. He loves his people and they love him. Love is always a possibility when power is set aside.

The Powerless Prophet

I have a friend who is a retired seminary professor. He has noticed that young ministers seldom realize that it is impossible to simultaneously be prophetic and hold a position of power. The prophet must not be concerned about how his message will affect his ability to rule. Yet many ministers are afraid to declare what the Bible says about prominent evils of our time because they know their church members will become angry.

I often speak at ministerial conferences and at seminaries, and am usually asked to address social issues. So I talk about what the Bible says about racism, the poor, war and peace, capital punishment, and other controversial subjects. Inevitably, some preacher will come up to me afterward to comment, "If I verbalized some of the things you said today, I'd be without a pulpit." I usually answer, "I know."

What the preacher fails to recognize is that I can speak as I do because there's no way my audience can get back at me. Other than choosing not to invite me back, which is often the case, those to whom I speak cannot take anything from me. I am not dependent on them, so they cannot strip me of my symbols of office. Because I have nothing to lose, I am free to say what I believe the Scripture teaches. Powerlessness is a condition that frees a person to be prophetic.

I want to emphasize that being the pastor of a local church does not preclude the possibility of being prophetic or preaching on controversial issues. However, I must admit that combining the two is difficult. If a pastor is going to attempt this—and to be faithful to God he must—then he should do so in a spirit of meekness. Too often the congregation is turned off not by what the pastor is saying but by the manner in which he says it. When he speaks like a demagogue or proclaims his message with arrogance, he will inevitably encounter strong resistance from his listeners. If he acts as if his word is the final interpretation of Scripture, or as if he alone understands the biblical message, his hearers will turn deaf ears to him.

However, should he approach his congregation in humility, conveying that what he is about to say regarding current issues comes from his own study and understanding of Scripture and that he is open to correction if he is wrong, he might find his congregation more open than he would expect. His message would be an invitation to his listeners to discuss contemporary problems in the light of the Word of God. He should communicate that while the crucial matter under discussion is too important to be ignored, he is not the final authority on the subject. The congregation should see him as one who is faithfully struggling to proclaim the whole counsel of God. They should feel invited to join him in the struggle so that together they might begin to grasp what God wants them to know about this issue.

When a preacher does not confront his congregation from a position of power, he will be amazed at how open the members can be. When members of the congregation sense that the message is coming from someone who loves them, rather than from someone who condemns or despises them for their "limited vision," they may grant him a high level of receptivity. If I could write a beatitude, it would be:

> Blessed are you when men reject you
> because you declare the Word of God;
> but cursed are you if they reject God's Word
> because of the way you declare it.

Pastors must learn that they cannot dominate their congregations or function like religious power brokers. To demand compliance with their views is just not Christlike. This is not to suggest that there is no room for stern condemnation or bold proclamation. However, in time of controversy, the declaration to a congregation which begins, "Thus saith the Lord," should be delivered only after much prayer and fasting. It should be uttered with fear and trembling. And it should come only after every possible approach in love has been rejected.

Lone Rangers for Jesus

The destructiveness of pastoral power was horribly exemplified in the saga of Jim Jones and the People's Temple. The world was shocked when, under his influence and command, hundreds of his followers committed suicide in the jungles of Guyana. Yet those who have traced the history and development of his leadership, and the movement it generated, have many positive things to say about Jim Jones.

His early theology and behavior, though somewhat unorthodox, could hardly be considered socially deviant. His preaching was helpful to many troubled people. There are those who testified that through Jones, and the People's Temple, they were rescued from lifestyles which would have spelled their doom. Drug addicts were delivered from dependency on heroin; alcoholics found release from their sickness; and prostitutes rediscovered a sense of dignity. The stories of people who were helped by Jim Jones go on and on. Through the People's Temple he had an extensive social ministry, providing assistance for poor people, exercising a positive influence on the political system, and even encouraging economic development in Third World countries.

However, with his growing successes came growing power. As his movement grew, people gave him more and more adoration for his accomplishments. As his power expanded, Jones gained more control over his followers. At first they willingly complied with his orders; in time, they found they had no other choice. Those who opposed him discovered that he could have them punished and, if need be, murdered. Love turned into fear as Jones changed into a powerful demagogue.

This is what happens when a leader's power goes unchecked, when he has no one to whom he is obligated or responsible.

With no one to correct him, he will inevitably develop a messianic complex and suffer from megalomania. While no pastor in a normal church situation is likely to imitate Jim Jones, many do find themselves corrupted by their own sense of power. In too many cases, a pastor will operate beyond the control of deacons or elders, and without restraint from the congregation. When this happens, it is possible for him to gradually destroy himself.

We all have diabolical tendencies and perverted desires. But fortunately, most of us do not have the power to express them. Society prevents us from carrying out these impulses which lie beneath our outward appearance of morality and propriety. However, if these societal restraints are removed, it is not long before we begin to evidence cruelties and lustful cravings which render us extremely dangerous.

I know of one prominent minister who was a dynamic preacher and creative leader. His church grew by leaps and bounds until it was one of the largest and most influential in his city. Because of his charisma, his congregation was in awe of him and never dared oppose him. His lay leadership were not strong enough to stand up to him, even when they knew he was wrong. So his power went unchecked and little by little brought about his destruction. He began to act as though the rules and regulations which he taught for others did not apply to him. He became involved in an extramarital sexual affair which eventually led to his divorce. When his behavior became so outlandish that his congregation finally rose up and wrested his power and his pulpit away from him, he acted surprised. He had become so deluded by power that he thought he could do anything and not suffer negative consequences from his actions.

I believe every pastor should have a small select group of people to whom he is willing to submit himself and be responsible. He should allow this support group to evaluate his lifestyle and call him to repentance when this is needed. He should be yielded to the counsel of this group and willing to obey their directives.

Whenever an individual Christian finds himself functioning as a Lone Ranger for Jesus, he becomes dangerous. This is why the Apostle James instructed Christians to be in fellowship with a group of believers, to whom we can confess our sins and who will provide discipline when needed (James 5:16). Without restraints from fellow Christians, we are in danger of giving vent to our worst tendencies, with the possibility of devastating results.

Powerful Missionaries

Power problems are particularly evident among missionaries. Missionary service can be a means of achieving power if it creates dependency among the nationals. If things are done for people which they can do for themselves, the people become subservient to those who serve them. Too many missionaries have maneuvered themselves into positions of power over the people they seek to serve, by doing more than they should for those people. Sometimes they have deliberately sought to buy the allegiance of the people by providing schools, medical care, and economic opportunities.

After the missionaries had done so much, the nationals found themselves in a state of obligation. They felt they owed it to the missionaries to do what they were told and to believe what they were told to believe. Such people quickly turn away from Christianity when the social and economic benefits derived from submission to the missionaries are no longer forthcoming.

On some foreign mission fields, the missionaries have withdrawn to allow indigenous Christian leaders to take over the churches. However, this needs to happen in many more places. Yet in case after case, missionaries do not seem able to let go of their power. They argue that the indigenous people are not capable of handling roles of leadership, or that they need more training to ensure the continuance of an effective program. Even when such missionaries try to turn over their work to indigenous leaders, they hover in the background, ready to seize control if anything goes wrong.

Even more pathetic is to watch missionaries who have learned to enjoy positions of power on the field return home to America and endeavor to live normal lives. Often they cannot make the adjustment. They cannot tolerate being ordinary church members in a local church, nor can they live relatively void of power. They become critical of their pastor, try to demonstrate superiority over other church members, and sometimes become such malcontents that the rest of the church is happy if they leave. They long to return to the mission field where they can be the powerful ones who are in charge.

In the 1960s, many nations of Africa gained independence and brought an end to colonialism. They began to express a nationalistic spirit that resulted in their rejection of foreign influences. Consequently, many missionaries were asked to leave these African countries. Mission schools and hospitals were nationalized and the missionaries who remained were often forced into roles subservient to national church leaders. There were predictions that results of a century of missionary efforts would collapse and that Christianity in Africa would experience great reversals.

But just the opposite happened. During the last 15 years, the number of Christians on the African continent south of the Sahara Desert has increased from 10 million to over 70 million. According to one estimate, there are 60,000 new members added to African churches every week. African churches are now sending out missionaries who are experiencing great success. It seems that the loss of power by American missionaries did not bring the decline of the African churches but, rather, assisted their growth. More was accomplished in the missionaries' loss of power than would have been possible had they held on to it. Today, many of these missionaries are discovering an unanticipated joy in working in the servant roles. They are learning through experience what the Bible has declared:

> Jesus called them together and said, "You know that the rulers of the Gentiles lord it over them, and their high officials exercise authority over them. Not so with you. Instead, whoever wants to become great among you must be your servant, and whoever wants to be first must be your slave—just as the Son of man did not come to be served, but to serve, and to give His life as a ransom for many" (Matthew 20:25–28).

Following Christ

Recalcitrant church leaders learn the hard way that they often do more harm than good through the practice of power. Pastors need to realize that even power exercised in a benevolent manner can stymie the spiritual growth of the congregation and have destructive effects on the life of the church.

Jesus reserved some of His harshest words for religious leaders of His day who lorded themselves over others and delighted in their power. "Woe to you Pharisees, because you love the most important seats in the synagogues and greetings in the marketplaces" (Luke 11:43).

He warned His disciples that it must never be that way with them! "Not so with you. Instead, whoever wants to become great among you must be your servant" (Matthew 20:26).

As I reflect upon my years as a pastor, I recall the pain and suffering I endured. Some of the struggles and conflicts made my life miserable. Yet when I reevaluate those difficulties, I see how many of them were the result of my own power plays. I wanted my way and had no patience with people who would not yield to me. Many of my plans for the church were good and probably would have increased the church's outreach.

However, in trying to force my will on others, my efforts became counterproductive. By operating from a position of power, I alienated the very people I was trying to serve. When they reacted negatively to my best plans and most creative visions, I was reduced to a bitter, frustrated person who hated being a minister.

It is pathetic to see people who, in order to do the will of God, resort to the methods of Satan. Force and power do not bring the kingdom of God.

6
Sanctified Power

With a Church Like This, Who Needs Satan?

The Apostle Paul was concerned about a power struggle going on between two leaders of the Philippian church, Euodia and Syntyche. These two women had been co-workers with Paul in establishing Christian work in Philippi.

Unfortunately, Euodia and Syntyche had been seduced into playing power games. Each was struggling for a dominant position within the church and had gathered her own group of supporters. This struggle for power that threatened to divide the Philippian church was one of the matters prompting Paul to write the Epistle to the Philippians.

Paul pleaded with Euodia and Syntyche to be of the *same mind* (Philippians 4:2). This wording was used earlier in the letter, as Paul wrote:

> Make my joy complete by being of the same mind, maintaining the same love, united in spirit, intent on one purpose.
> Do nothing from selfishness or empty conceit, but with humility of mind let each of you regard one another as more important than himself (2:2–3, NASB).

He had urged the entire church to use Christ as a model.

> Your attitude should be the same as that of Christ Jesus: who, being in very nature God, did not consider equality with God something to be grasped, but made Himself nothing, taking on the very nature of a servant, being made in human likeness. And being found in appearance as a man, He humbled Himself and became obedient to death—even death on a cross! (2:5–8)

Paul pointed out that Jesus set aside His power and glory when He entered history as a baby in a manger. He grew up to be an obedient servant who was willing to humble Himself for the sake of others. He did not break into history with a conquering army, or establish Himself as a ruling monarch. Instead, He chose to be a suffering servant, and was even willing to surrender Himself to death on the cross. The style of Jesus was a contrast to the power-seeking of Euodia and Syntyche. He set aside power to sacrificially express love. Euodia and Syntyche set aside love to engage in a power struggle.

From the earliest days of Christianity up to the present, the church has been threatened by power plays. Sometimes members are jealous of the power of the pastor and work to undermine him. In more cases than I would care to cite, church members have sought to break a pastor and bring him under their control. These attacks take a variety of forms. They can weaken the pastor through constant criticism. Instead of praying for the pastor, they prey on him, picking on every little thing they can find. They ridicule him to other church members. They work hard to diminish his stature in the eyes of the congregation.

When I was a young pastor, there was a woman in my church who was out to get me. She criticized the way I preached, the way I dressed, and the way I greeted people after the service. She demonstrated the ludicrous extremes to which she was willing to go by claiming that during the communion service I ate the bread too quickly. She had been able to dominate the former pastor and was angry because she could not dominate me. I did not help the situation, since I was determined to show her she could not push me around. I was out to prove that I was in control of the church and that she could not stop me. Between the two of us, the church suffered greatly.

In most cases, members who struggle to gain control of a church are people who have a sense of powerlessness in their everyday lives. Perhaps they feel put down at their jobs or find themselves dominated at home. In one way or another, they feel they have been diminished by others. They find that within the church they are allowed to assert themselves and even be aggressive. They discover that the church provides them with opportunities to engage in power games they are incapable of playing in the world.

Most churches are so desperate for the support of their members that it is easy for power hungry people to manipulate this dependence into an opportunity. By threatening to withhold their financial support, they can pressure the board to urge the pastor to comply with their wishes. In a small church, the simple threat not to attend services can blackmail a pastor into yielding to such demands. I often wished I had thousands of members in my congregation, just so that I could be indifferent to threats from the kind of people who told me that if I did not comply with what they wanted they would go to worship elsewhere. I wanted to be the pastor of a church so large that such people would know their absence would not even be noticed.

St. Paul had to constantly face up to challenges to his authority from people who wanted to replace him in the leadership structure of the church. There were people who questioned his qualifications, others who questioned his background and spirituality, and still others who raised doubts about his zeal. Paul answered his detractors by claiming that any outward comparison between himself and other church workers would show him to be superior.

> I myself have reasons for such confidence. If anyone else thinks he has reasons to put confidence in the flesh, I have more: circumcised on the eighth day, of the people of Israel, of the tribe of Benjamin, a Hebrew of Hebrews; in regard to the law, a Pharisee (Philippians 3:4–6).

However, Paul did not believe that such things were of any significance. He looked upon his list of credits with contempt and made it clear that the only thing that really mattered was his relationship with Christ. "But whatever was to my profit I now consider loss for the sake of Christ" (Philippians 3:7).

Paul based his authority on how much he had suffered for Christ. Seeking the role of the suffering servant rather than the role of power broker or office holder is the goal of the Christian. Paul made it clear that within the church, people should seek to suffer for others rather than rule them. "Carry each other's burdens, and in this way you will fulfill the law of Christ" (Galations 6:2). He criticized all power struggles in the church and allowed for only one kind of competition, to outdo one another in love. He encouraged each member of the church to put other people above himself and to render more service to others than was rendered to him.

> Do not take revenge, my friends, but leave room for God's wrath, for it is written: "It is mine to avenge; I will repay," says the Lord. On the contrary: "If your enemy is hungry, feed him; if he is thirsty, give him something to drink. In doing this, you will heap burning coals on his head." Do not be overcome by evil, but overcome evil with good (Romans 12:19–21).

Many church members think they can obligate God. They believe that if they do enough good works, God will owe them salvation. They can't get it through their heads that salvation is given only to those who know they have no power to obtain it for themselves. We are saved by grace, not by good works. Salvation is a gift; therefore, no one can boast that he did anything to earn it.

> For it is by grace you have been saved, through faith—and this is not from yourselves, it is the gift of God—not by works, so that no one can boast (Ephesians 2:8–9).

People who are in love with power cannot handle this. They want to determine their destinies through their own efforts. They want to have control over their lives. Such people have a hard time realizing that we are saved by rendering ourselves powerless before God, by surrendering to God and allowing Him to do what we are unable to do. Jesus saves those who come to Him in their weakness. Those who think they have the power to earn their salvation through good works do not stand a chance.

Magic in the Church

I am increasingly concerned that so many people seem to be playing manipulative games with God. Bronislaw Malinowski, one of the great anthropologists of the twentieth century, differentiates between magic and religion. Magic is a system in which people endeavor to gain control over spiritual forces in order that they might obtain what they want. Magic is a means of gaining the power to dictate what the spiritual forces do. Contrariwise, religion is a system wherein people surrender themselves to spiritual forces so that they might be servants through whom those spiritual forces can minister in the world.

According to Malinowski's definitions, there is a great deal of magic in the church which passes itself off as religion. People are looking for the right formula to get their prayers answered.

There are those who try to bargain with God. They offer to do certain things for God to obligate Him to do certain things for them.

A young man at the college where I teach was dating a coed on our campus. She did not seem particularly interested in him, so he came to my office to talk about what he should do so that she would love him. He suggested that prayer could make her turn to him. "After all," he said, "through prayer all things are possible." He wanted me to join him in his prayer efforts because, "the prayers of a faithful man availeth much" (James 5:16). I was flattered to think that he considered me a faithful man, but I could not go along with his scheme. I had to ask him whether he was surrendered to the will of God, whatever that might be, or if he was endeavoring to pressure God to fulfill his own personal wishes. He believed in a God who could be manipulated for one's own purposes and who would manipulate others upon request. I had a hard time convincing him to the contrary.

Manipulative Prayer

On a less selfish level I have to raise some serious questions about the commonly accepted notion that if we pray enough, God will bring certain people to salvation. I could tell you of many mothers on guilt trips because their sons or daughters have not come to the Lord. They were led to believe that if they prayed more and lived more in accord with God's will, their children would be saved. While I would not for one moment discourage prayer for the lost, I do not want prayer reduced to a magical formula that produces guaranteed results for the prayer. We are all aware of parents who have desperately and constantly prayed for their wayward children only to have their children remain unresponsive to the Lord. Sometimes such parents wrongly condemn themselves and think that if they had been more spiritual and more diligent in their pleadings to God, their children would be saved.

There are problems with this kind of theology. First, it presupposes that God does not want to save the child and will only be persuaded if the parents keep after Him enough. Such a thought dishonors God who does not want anyone to perish (2 Peter 3:9). He loves that wayward child more than the parents do and is more brokenhearted over the child's rejection of His love and will than the father or mother could ever be.

Also, this kind of theology assumes that God will force people into compliance with His will if we can just persuade Him to really want to. This is not God's way. He loves, He pleads, He entreats, but He does not force. People have not been created as puppets who can be controlled by the prayers of others. Ultimately, the wayward child must freely choose to give his or her life to Christ.

What Prayer Does

I do not want to leave the impression that prayer does not accomplish anything or that it is without effect on the lost. I earnestly believe that intercessory prayer surrounds the person with the love of God in a special way. Through prayer we do not so much manipulate God to do our will as we become surrendered instruments through whom God's love can move those who are dear to us. We usually think of prayer as a means whereby we reach another person through God. But I am suggesting that prayer is a way in which God can flow through us to that other person. We can all be sending agents for the love of God. I am convinced that in prayer we become channels through whom the passionate love of God flows and engulfs other persons. The more we pray and the more people we get to pray, the more channels there are for the infinite love of our Lord to flow to, surround, and invade the person we hold up in prayer.

Consider how Jesus prayed. He was not out to change His Father's will, but rather to become a surrendered instrument through whom the Father could do great and wonderful things. Jesus said to the Father, "Not as I will, but as Thou wilt " (Matthew 26:39). Jesus was not trying to get the Father to do what He did not plan to do until asked. Rather, Jesus was offering Himself up to the Father as a perfect instrument through whom the heavenly Father could move into the lives of needy people. Jesus was constantly praying and fasting. The Father could do more through us if we, through prayer and fasting, would become the kinds of instruments and channels God needs to move into the lives of others.

Nevertheless, prayer does not produce automatic results. The persons for whom we pray may, as a result of prayer, be more surrounded by the passionate love of God than would have been the case if we had not prayed. The presence of God may be engulfing such a person in a way that would not be the case if we were not willing vessels through whom God can reveal Himself to them. The enticing beauty of God may be more clearly revealed to them because God has us as instruments to get to them. But even with all this, the persons for whom we pray can still say no. That is why there is a hell, and that is why people go there—people who refuse to yield to the love of the beautiful Saviour whose presence has engulfed them through the prayers of the faithful.

I always remind those who pray earnestly for their unsaved friends and family members that Jesus Himself had family members who rejected Him. He had several brothers, but only a few came to acknowledge Him as Lord. The others, like many for whom we pray, rejected His pleading love. If Jesus would not override the rebellious wills of His own brothers, then we must not assume it will be otherwise with our brothers and sisters. We must pray for them, because it is through prayer that the loving presence of Christ can impact their lives and become dynamically real to them. But we cannot guarantee the salvation of loved ones through prayer, because prayer is not a manipulative magical power. Yet we need to realize that there is the possibility that they might not be saved if we do not pray.

I am aware of a variety of implications in what I am suggesting, but I am convinced that those implications are in accord with the will of God. First of all, if what I have said about prayer is valid, then we become participants with God in reaching the lost with the love of God. I believe this is what the Bible is saying when it states that we are workers together with God for the salvation of the lost (2 Corinthians 6:1). God invites us to be part of His plan for reaching the world. Our dignity and worth are enhanced infinitely by the awesome news that God wants to use us as instruments of His love, that He wants us to be vessels through whom His presence is experienced by those who need him.

I also realize that what I have said implies that the Father could do through us what He was able to do through Jesus. Once again I assert that this is exactly what the Scripture teaches. Jesus said as much Himself:

I tell you the truth, anyone who has faith in Me will do what I have been doing. He will do even greater things than these, because I am going to the Father (John 14:12).

No wonder the Epistle to the Romans says:

The Spirit Himself testifies with our spirit that we are God's children. Now if we are children, then we are heirs—heirs of God and co-heirs with Christ, if indeed we share in His sufferings in order that we may also share in His glory (Romans 8:16–17).

The time has come for us to turn away from that form of religiosity which Malinowski properly calls magic. Prayer must not be reduced to playing power games with God. True religion is not manipulating God but being surrendered to His will and to His service. In true religion God is able to use us to bless others. That is why James wrote in his epistle:

> Religion that God our Father accepts as pure and faultless is this: to look after orphans and widows in their distress and to keep oneself from being polluted by the world (James 1:27).

7
Glorious Authority

The Way the Kingdom Comes

During the first century of its existence, the church was basically a powerless movement. Its members were, for the most part, working-class people and slaves. The Apostle Paul wrote about the composition of the early church:

> Brothers, think of what you were when you were called. Not many of you were wise by human standards; not many were influential; not many were of noble birth. But God chose the foolish things of the world to shame the wise; God chose the weak things of the world to shame the strong. He chose the lowly things of this world and the despised things—and the things that are not—to nullify the things that are, so that no one may boast before Him (1 Corinthians 1:26–29).

These early followers of Jesus could hardly be called the movers and shakers of the Roman world. Nevertheless, the first century Christians did make a decisive difference among the people of their day. They won converts in great numbers. They sent missionaries to carry the Gospel to the far reaches of the empire. They challenged the morality of the existing social structures. Though the church commanded no armies, held no political power, it still was able to sufficiently threaten the lifestyle of the Roman Empire to warrant the wrath of its emperors.

In A.D. 312 the Christian church went through a major transition which changed its character. In that year, the Emperor Constantine gave positive recognition to Christianity and provided it with favored status so that Christianity became the official religion of the Roman Empire. From this dubious honor the church has not recovered yet. Under the favor of Constantine, the Christian church moved from being a despised, persecuted minority to the dominant religion of society. Its leaders were no longer renegades and outlaws, but persons who could and would wield power.

The general consensus of church historians is that when Christianity allied itself with the power of the state, it entered into a period of corruption and disintegration, gradually losing much of its moral authority and most of its spiritual dynamic. The church was not meant to wield power; when it did, it betrayed its calling as an agent of love. As the church increased in power, it decreased in authority.

After Constantine, the church changed from a persecuted body of believers into a persecuting institution, often burning at the stake those who deviated from its doctrines. The church was gradually transformed from a community which sent out missionaries to win the world to Christ into a crusading army that would march on the Arab world to bring death and suffering to millions. The church failed to understand that it would be corrupted by power because power contradicts love. Love is what the pure church is all about.

Moral Majority

Unfortunately, the church has not learned from the tragedies of history and, consequently, has frequently repeated its mistakes. Recently, many evangelical Christians have yielded to the temptations of power, forming themselves into a major political movement called the Moral Majority. They figured that if they could get their own people elected to political offices they could control the decision-making processes of government. They thought that if they had political power they could force their will and morality on the entire American public.

I am not here debating the rightness of the positions taken by the leaders of the Moral Majority, nor am I condemning their desire to create a better America. Actually, very few Christians oppose the basic platform of the Moral Majority. Their emphasis on family life is desperately needed. Their condemnation of the declining commitment to ethical standards is timely. Their indignation over the imposition of secular humanist values in the educational system is needed.

What concerns me is the method they employ to bring about changes in society. It seems to me that the leaders of the Moral Majority have been seduced into using power in their efforts. They are depending on the strength of the state to enforce their will. I believe this is a serious mistake that will, in the long run, hurt the witness of the church and significantly diminish its authority.

One of my friends, who is an ardent member of the Moral Majority, correctly points out that I am only now criticizing the use of power by Christian organizations, and that I had nothing to say about such methods when Christian liberals used political power to implement their programs for social change during the 1960s. He points out that the leaders of the National Council of Churches applied all kinds of political pressure in their efforts to pass civil rights legislation. Without doubt, liberal church leaders affirmed the legitimacy of using political power to end the war in Vietnam. My friend claims that using political power to pursue Christian causes was never questioned by the spokespersons of mainline Christianity until they realized that conservative Christians could play the power games too. In short, he finds it hypocritical for liberals to push their programs through the use of political power and then criticize the conservatives in the church when they adopt the same means.

My friend is right in his criticism. While I am a conservative Christian in matters of theology, I tend to hold many political views which my critics consider liberal. My friend correctly notes that I had nothing to say when the leaders of the National Council of Churches used all the pressure tactics available in their efforts to champion civil rights for blacks and to bring about what they believed to be a more progressive society. However, I have become an outspoken critic of power tactics when they are employed by the Moral Majority. All I can say is that I did not give much thought to a biblical perspective on power until it was used effectively by this group.

My concern now is with any church group that chooses to function like a political party. Whether that group be to the right or to the left of the political spectrum makes no difference. The National Council of Churches upsets me when it exercises political power and the Moral Majority upsets me for the same reasons. Whenever church groups play power games, they are not being faithful to their calling, nor to the Bible.

World Changers

I am *not* suggesting that the people of God should refrain from changing the world. Quite the opposite. I am absolutely convinced that Jesus saves us from sin primarily to make us into world changers. As we read through the New Testament, we quickly realize that Jesus did not die on the cross simply to save us from hell and get us into heaven, although His death on the cross makes both of these things possible. Jesus also died to make us into a holy people whom He could use to change His world. Through those who are yielded to His will, He wants to invade all parts of the social order with His love. Through those who are possessed by His Holy Spirit, He seeks to challenge the principalities and powers of this world—governments, economic structures, the media, educational institutions—to bring them under His domain.

> Then the end will come, when He hands over the kingdom to God the Father after He has destroyed all dominion, authority and power. For He must reign until He has put His enemies under His feet (1 Corinthians 15:23–25).

Christians are motivated by a divine imperative to be agents of transformation, instruments for social change, and participants in God's revolution. This is not a reworked version of the old social gospel which imagined that we, through our efforts, could change a messed-up world into the kingdom of God. Instead, this is a call to participate with God in the work He is doing in this world, with the realization that the kingdom comes with the Second Coming of Christ. He begins the work of transforming His world through those of us who are yielded to His will, and he completes that good work when He Himself returns to earth in glory (Philippians 1:6).

For me there is no question but that we are to be involved with what happens to this world. We are to be the salt of the earth that permeates all areas of life with the love of God. We are to be agents that effect change in society in such a way that we are analogous to what leaven does to dough in the process of making bread (Matthew 5:13; 13:33).

How Do We Change the World?
If we are to be at work in the world in the name of Christ, the question that concerns us is How? How do we change the world? By what means do we seek to alter the structure of society? In what ways do we give expression to the love of God in the social institutions of the modern world?

A few years ago some of my Eastern College students became very upset with a multinational corporation that was producing sugar in the Dominican Republic. We decided to buy stock in the corporation, enabling us to go to stockholders' meetings and there endeavor to champion the changes we thought necessary for the health and well-being of the Dominican people. We believed that the land the corporation was using to grow sugar should be used to grow food for the hungry population of that developing nation, and that the company should abandon its growing involvement in the Dominican economy.

At first we joined forces with others who had concerns similar to ours. We attempted to contact other stockholders in the corporation so that we would represent a significant block of shareholder votes at the meeting. We thought we could force the company to accept our position.

Subsequently, we not only failed, but my students and I went through a process of reevaluation as to whether we were going about this effort to change corporation policy in the right manner.

We began to reflect on whether Jesus would try to *force* a company to do what is right. We asked whether He would employ coercion as a means of bringing about justice. After much discussion and consideration, we changed our tactics. We went to the executives in the corporation as friends and asked them if they would be willing to work along with us to improve the life and conditions of the Dominican people.

Much to our surprise, and somewhat to our embarrassment, we found that the leaders of the corporation were not as we had imagined them to be. They were basically decent people who wanted to do what was right. And once we abandoned an attempt to coerce them into conformity with our ideas of justice, they were quite willing to reconsider their activities.

They readily admitted they were doing many things that did not serve the best interests of the Dominican people. And they were willing to change their practices to whatever degree was possible. They demonstrated to us in a very clear manner that they wanted to have a just and equitable business.

One afternoon I received a telephone call from one of the executives of the corporation. He told me that the following day they would be making an announcement to the press which would demonstrate their strong desire to improve the life of the Dominican people. He told me that the company would be testing the soil they were using for growing sugar, and that all the land which could be used to grow food to feed the Dominican people would be utilized for this purpose. Only land that could not be used to grow food for indigenous consumption would be utilized for growing sugar.

Furthermore, I was told, the company had committed itself to investing more than $100 million on social, economic, and educational projects aimed at improving the quality of life of the Dominican people.

This company is the Gulf and Western Corporation. It was originally listed by some social activists as one of the ten most immoral corporations in the world. Whether that designation was ever justified, I cannot say. But this I do know—Gulf and Western has become a shining example of a corporation that is trying to exercise moral responsibility in a Third World nation.

What is important to our discussion is that the leaders of this corporation did not respond to force and coercion. They would not be intimidated. But when approached in friendship and love, they were more than responsive to reasonable requests to effect change in their policies.

There are those who think that without coercive power it is impossible to get anything done in today's world. They are convinced that the powerless cannot expect to make the world better or worse. But then such people have given very little consideration to the style of Jesus.

Our Lord had power sufficient to force all of us to our knees, to destroy all the evil in society, and make all things right again. Yet, He chose not to save the world through the exercise of power but rather to change it through His love. In Philippians 2, we read how Christ who had all the power of God—because He was God and is God—set aside His power and glory and chose to enter history as a humble baby in a manger. Christ emptied Himself of all the power and glory of the Father and took upon Him the weaknesses that we associate with living in the flesh.

The story of Bethlehem was not meant to be a sentiment that would touch our hearts for the Christmas season, although it does just that. It was meant to describe the extent to which Christ was willing to go in His effort to save us from sin and bring salvation to His world. He came in the weakness of flesh and lived among us as a servant. His was a life of simple obedience to the will of His Father, even to dying on a cross when that was asked of Him. He confronted the powerful demonic hosts not with a blazing display of His own power but with love.

On Calvary's cross we see what the power of Satan can do. There we observe the demonic nature of political and religious power. The Roman governor and Hebrew king, on the one hand, and priests and scribes of the religious system, on the other, conspired together to destroy God. All of their claims to be agents of goodness were stripped away on the cross, as principalities and powers were exposed to be the power hungry agents they really are. Christ confronted them, not with the power which was at His disposal, but rather with the awesome splendor of His love. The cross displays the depraved nature of demonic powers as expressed through the rulers of the age; it also displays the love of God in its most perfect form. On the cross, power confronted love; on Good Friday, it looked as though power had won. But the demonic hosts counted the spoils of victory too quickly. Two days later the stone was rolled away as love incarnate was resurrected. History would from then on recognize that love is greater than power and ultimately will triumph over it. The resurrection is evidence that love is greater than all the power that man and Satan together can ever muster.

The resurrected Christ still endeavors to effect change through love. He does not coerce us into His kingdom, but lovingly entreats us. He does not force His way into our lives, but instead says, "Behold I stand at the door and knock; if any one hears my voice and opens the door, I will come in to him, and will dine with him, and he with Me (Revelation 3:20, NASB).

One of my favorite hymns, "He Could Have Called Ten Thousand Angels," so wonderfully explains the style of Jesus. As He hung on the Roman cross, the Pharisees and priests mocked Him, "If You are the Son of God, come down from the cross and we shall believe" (Matthew 27:40–42, NASB). There is no question but that He could have done that. What is more, He could have snapped His fingers and ten thousand angels in shining raiment would have been instantaneously at His side. But that wasn't His style; love kept Him obediently nailed to the cross. That was an hour to reveal the love of God. Another hour would come when He would unleash His power.

Many Christians who would say Amen to all of this still fail to see how the style of Jesus expresses a style we might employ today in our mission to change the world. They do not understand that Jesus established a pattern which He expects all of His followers to imitate.

Civil Rights Marchers

Among those in recent times who have dared to imitate the style of Jesus was Martin Luther King. In his efforts to bring social justice to American blacks, he proposed civil rights marches from Selma to Montgomery, Alabama on two consecutive weekends. On live television we watched as the marchers tried to cross a bridge just outside Selma, only to have their way barred by Sheriff Clark and his deputies. The marchers were told to turn back, but the response was, "We've come too far to turn back now."

A second warning was given and with that the civil rights marchers went on their knees in prayer. After a countdown, Clark and his followers charged the kneeling demonstrators, bashing their heads with billy clubs and subjecting them to the terror of vicious police dogs. We Americans saw it all happen. We witnessed the brutalizing of people who were asking for nothing more than their inalienable rights as Americans. It was heartbreaking and shocking to behold. But even as it happened, something inside of me seemed to say, "They've won! The civil rights marchers have won!"

Those who do not know the ways of the Lord would not understand how a bunch of battered civil rights workers who had just been beaten with clubs and bitten by dogs could be called winners. To the uninitiated, Sheriff Clark with his helmeted soldiers and shield-wielding army seemed to be the victor. He and his men had chased the civil rights marchers from the bridge. The blood of those "uppity blacks" was all over the road. How could anybody consider the demonstrators the victors?

But then how many would ever understand the style of the One who promised that the first would be last and the last first? (Matthew 19:30) How could those who do not know the story of Jesus possibly realize that He was born to lift up the lowly and to bring down the powerful? (Luke :52) On the bridge outside of Selma, a victory had been won through weakness; a battle had been won by love.

Moral Authority
Another modern-day example of how the style of Jesus can effect change in the world can be seen in Mother Teresa. She commands no army, she sits in no parliament, she has no

wealth; and yet when she speaks, the world listens. Mother Teresa possesses no power in this world, but she does possess great authority. Her authority has been established by her willingness to sacrifice in the service of others. She has followed the example of her Saviour and has become a suffering servant.

About His sacrificial death, Jesus said, "I, if I be lifted up from the earth, will draw all men to Myself (John 12:32, NASB). By that He meant that His death on the cross would exercise a magnetic effect on men. He would not have to force people to accept Him and His message. His sacrifice would attract them and He would have authority because of His cross. Men are by nature awed by self-sacrifice and they respond with gratitude to those who will sacrifice on their behalf.

Mother Teresa follows the example of Jesus and, consequently, has some of the same attraction and authority that people find in the crucified Lord. The more one gives to others in love, sacrifices for the well-being of others, and suffers for the cause of righteousness, the more one grows in authority. Mother Teresa finds herself in possession of great authority because she has done all of these things. The world is challenged by her and others like her in spite of the fact, or perhaps because of the fact, that they never sought power.

The members of the Moral Majority and the leaders of the National Council of Churches have yet to learn the lessons of Christ and of history regarding power. They fail to see that when Christianity became the Moral Majority under Constantine, the church was corrupted and Christianity lost its authority. They fail to see that in resorting to power plays and the use of political force to promote their social programs, they lose their ability to speak with the authority of God. Religious power groups end up being treated like all other political parties— with cynicism and fear.

Political Compromise

In 1976 I was a candidate for the U.S. Congress from the fifth district of Pennsylvania. I had a rather simplistic perspective on the things wrong with America and thought I knew how to straighten out the mess. It seemed to me that the problems of the country were the result of having bad people in office. All that was needed to set things right was to elect good people to replace the bad ones. Needless to say, I considered myself to be one of the goodies and my opponent to be one of the baddies.

In the course of formulating this political philosophy, I had failed to ask a simple question, "What made the bad guys bad?" Undoubtedly, the baddies had good motivations when they first ran for office. Though not necessarily Christians, they probably espoused high ideals and had dreams of doing good for America and all of humanity. What went wrong? Where did the dreams die? Why did so many of these people degenerate into political hacks interested only in holding on to their offices?

The answers to such questions lie in the nature of power and the way it corrupts those who possess it. There is no possibility of holding on to power without compromise. Those in political office know that it is difficult, if not impossible, to press for what they believe is right in every case. Politicians know that the way to stay in office is to yield on some issues in order to gain support on others. Every time a candidate takes a strong stand on an issue, he alienates some people. Therefore, he tries to speak out on as few issues as possible. Candidates try to remain ambiguous because clarity hurts their chances of winning.

For instance, trying to nail down the average candidate on his position on abortion is most difficult. He will evade or say he has not yet made up his mind on the issue. Perhaps he will double-talk his contituency by saying something like, "I am personally opposed to abortion, but I question whether there should be a public policy on this matter." The pro-life supporters have learned how to keep politicians from weasling out of the question. They say, "If abortion is murdering a human being, then it isn't enough to say that one is personally opposed to it but would not like to see laws enacted to prohibit murder." The pro-choice people are equally adamant as they ask, "Do you believe that women should have the right to determine their own sexual destinies?" No wonder most politicians say no more on this issue than is absolutely necessary. They know that no matter how they answer, they antagonize part of their constituency.

The same kind of ambiguity is expressed when candidates are asked about social welfare programs for the poor. Particular candidates may be personally disposed to taking a strong stand for cutting military spending and putting more money into low-cost housing programs for the elderly, advantages for the handicapped, and job training programs for the unemployed. Yet in spite of their own convictions, they will tend to take stands on these issues which are in accord with the inclinations of their voters. Often they will poll their constituencies in order to get a clear picture of what positions would gain the most support.

When I was a candidate for the U.S. Congress, I was once asked if I would vote in accord with my constituency or with my conscience, if what I believed on a particular issue differed from what the people in my district believed. I responded by saying that I would vote in accord with my convictions, even if that meant that I would be opposed to most of the voters. I would listen to the arguments and cases made by concerned citizens and would be open to changing my mind if I could be convinced I was wrong. But, after all was said and done, I would have to vote in accord with what I believed was right and in accord with God's will, even if the polls showed that the people who had elected me had an opposite opinion.

I went on to explain that when Jesus was on trial, Pilate knew that Jesus was innocent and even announced to the crowd, "I find no fault in Him" (Luke 23:4, 14). But Pilate did not rule in accord with his conscience. Instead, he took a poll of his constituency. He asked the crowd, "What shall I do with Jesus?" (Matthew 27:22) And the crowd yelled, "Crucify Him." Pilate then voted in accord with his constituency rather than following what he knew to be right. He knew that to hold power he had to have support from the people, so he took a position which would please them. Too often, down through the years, politicians have followed the example of Pilate and have crucified Jesus anew.

Authority Without Power

The only people who can afford the luxury of being steadfast in their convictions are the powerless. The powerless have nothing to lose. There is nothing that can be taken from them. Those who don't want power can dare to live and act in a way that is consistent with their beliefs because there is nothing to be gained through compromise. That is why the members of the early church lived with such joyful abandon in the face of the principalities and powers and rulers of this world. They had given up power in favor of love and "perfect love casteth out fear" (1 John 4:18). Those who do not seek power are the ones who are most free to speak the truth, even when the truth is unpopular.

Recently I was asked to deliver an address to a group of political science professors from Christian colleges. The meeting was held in Washington, D.C. and was sponsored by the Christian College Coalition. I chose as my topic, "Authority and Power in Social Change." I explained that by my definition, *power* was the ability to make others do your will even if they would choose not to; and *authority* was the ability to get others to want to do your will because they recognize that what you ask is legitimate and right. I went on to set forth my belief that when power increases, authority decreases. I explained that with authority there is no need to control people, because they want to follow you. On the other hand, if you must resort to power to get people to do what you ask, you lack authority; even though you are obeyed, you will not be regarded as a legitimate ruler.

I did not realize that in the audience was a political exile from the Philippines. This man had been a senator and the leader of the opposition party to President Marcos. He had been imprisoned because of his outspoken opposition to many of the policies of the Marcos regime, particularly as those policies resulted in the violation of human rights. Marcos had slated him for execution, but President Jimmy Carter of the U.S. intervened on his behalf and saved him from death. This young senator developed a severe case of cancer and would have died in prison had not President Carter once again intervened, this time asking President Marcos to allow the political prisoner to come to the United States for special medical treatment. Marcos yielded to the request on the condition that the senator would return to jail in the Philippines following his medical care in a prominent Boston hospital. When I met him after my lecture in Washington, I learned that he had completed the treatments, and in accord with his promise, was planning to return to jail in the Philippines within two weeks.

I could see that this Filipino leader was deeply impressed by what I had said. When I asked him why he so much appreciated the lecture, he said, "You have given me hope. I know that when I return to my homeland I will be powerless; but you have helped me to see that I will have authority. What I say is right and people know it. What I believe to be true, I am willing to die for. I now believe I will have a great influence in the Philippines, even though I hold no power at all."

He is right, and I will be anxiously waiting to see how this once powerful leader affects the people in his native country. As a deeply committed Christian, faithful to his convictions, willing to suffer for what he believes, voluntarily presenting himself for imprisonment and possibly death, he will have an authority which will command a hearing. It may be that he will provide one more example of how someone with authority but no power can accomplish more than someone with power and no authority.

Political Power

Some of my friends who are Mennonites do not believe that Christians ought to hold political office. They reason that to hold office is to be in a position in which you can exercise power and force people to do what is right. They believe that Christians should never allow themselves to be in the position of governing by power.

From what I have set forth up to this point, it would be reasonable to conclude that I agree with my Mennonite friends. On the one hand, I do and on the other, I do not. And in saying that, I sound just like the politicians I have criticized.

What the Mennonites say is essentially true. Nevertheless, there is a need for Christians to go into politics. While it may be dangerous to a Christian's personal well-being for him to hold power, it may be more dangerous for society if he, or someone like him, is not in office.

Charles de Gaulle once said, "Politics are too serious a matter to be left to the politicians." I agree. I am convinced that dedicated Christians should recognize that they are needed in political office. The alternative to their being there is dangerous.

Edmund Burke once said, "All that is necessary for the forces of evil to win in the world is for enough good men to do nothing." If political offices are filled only by those who have no commitment to God and who are devoid of the values inherent in the Bible, we will all suffer.

It is important for Christians in politics to realize that power inevitably has a corrupting influence on those who hold it and that they must be on constant vigil against this influence. They should see the holding of political power as a necessary evil which will exist as long as we live in a fallen world where sin must be contained and punished. Humanity is sinful, people are motivated by the lusts of the flesh, and there are destructive tendencies in all of us.

In the face of such facts, it is necessary that there be rulers who govern us with justice and with commitment to protect us from our own worst tendencies and traits (Romans 13:2–3). Christians should not avoid such responsibilities, even though they are aware of what power does to people. Christians who hold power should do so with great reluctance, realizing that Plato spoke the truth when he said, "Only those who do not desire power are fit to hold it." Christians who love power and thrill in the ecstacy that comes from dominating others must recognize that they are out of the will of God.

The Danger of Power
The danger of holding power is brilliantly set forth in the Bible. In the Old Testament, God told the Children of Israel that they would be better off without a political ruler. He urged them to let Him be their King. Jehovah tried to convince His people that He alone could be trusted with power and that He alone was able to resist its corrupting influence. He told them that if they had a king, like the other nations of the world, their king would oppress them and reduce them to slaves.

> Samuel told all the words of the Lord to the people who were asking him for a king. He said, "This is what the king who will reign over you will do: He will take your sons and make them serve with his chariots and horses, and they will run in front of his chariots. Some he will assign to be commanders of thousands and commanders of fifties, and others to plow his ground and reap his harvest, and still others to make weapons of war and

equipment for his chariots. He will take your daughters to be
perfumers and cooks and bakers. He will take the best of your
fields and vineyards and olive groves, and give them to his attendants. He will take a tenth of your grain and of your vintage
and give it to his officials and attendants. Your menservants and
maidservants and the best of your cattle and donkeys he will take
for his own use. He will take a tenth of your flocks, and you
yourselves will become his slaves. When that day comes, you will
cry out for relief from the king you have chosen, and the Lord
will not answer you in that day" (1 Samuel 8:10–18).

Unfortunately, the Jews did not heed the pleadings of Jehovah and continued to implore Him for a king. They viewed
having a king as a thing of prestige and wanted the same
symbols of power enjoyed by other nations. Jehovah eventually
gave them what they wanted and Israel was issued into the
trials and tribulations of which Jehovah had warned them. It is
important to note that the Bible gives ample evidence that even
the best of Israel's kings could not resist the corrupting effects
of power. Ultimately, each king in turn abused the power of his
office and had to be called to repentance.

It would be well for Christian leaders in our own day to keep
before them the stories of the monarchs of ancient Israel.
There was Saul who so longed to hold onto power that he was
ready to destroy the one whom God had anointed as his succes-
sor. Eventually, he sought out the services of a witch to find out
if he would survive as Israel's ruler (1 Samuel 28:7–25).

There was Solomon who began his reign with the best of
intentions by asking the Lord for wisdom so that he might rule
with justice. Yet, in spite of this wonderful beginning, Solomon
fell victim to the lusts of his flesh. As king, he had the power
to get what he wanted, and what he wanted destroyed him.

David must have been God's favorite king. He certainly was
the favorite of the Jews. In so many ways he sought to please
the Lord and in so many ways he did. But the most heroic and

wonderful stories about David tell of the days that preceded his donning the crown of Israel. After he became king, he too was seduced by power and abused the privilege of his office.

These are among the best of kings. The rest of biblical history records a succession of rulers of whom most were even more sinful and lacking the redeeming characteristics of these three. If even the great kings who found favor with the Lord left such a tragic account of their exercise of power, rulers of today would do well to take heed. There must be rulers, but those who hold such positions should do so with fear and trembling. Christians need to take up the offices of state, but with a caution which demonstrates a knowledge of what political power does to people.

8
The Terrible Cost of Conquering Love

Why God Withholds His Power

When it comes to power, nobody has more than God. The heavens declare His glory. All of nature gives evidence of what He can do. His word can command anything to come out of nothing. All things are held together by Him.

The knowledge of the power of God leads inevitably to the question of why God does not use His power as we feel He should. There are wars He could stop, and yet He allows them to grind on to their destructive conclusions. He could heal the sick and make the blind to see, and yet in most cases He does not. He is able to keep tragedies from happening and yet they do happen. He could feed all the hungry of the world and yet many starve.

If God is so powerful, why doesn't He make this the best of all possible worlds? Why doesn't He set things right? Why doesn't He abolish evil? It is not enough to say that it is not God's will that these evils be corrected; or that there are great lessons He is trying to teach us through such trials; or that such terrible events are part of some wonderful plan we will one day understand.

When the victims of tragedy, injustice, and absurd events ask the simple question, "Why?" these worn-out answers do not seem to suffice. We Christians try to make excuses for God so that He won't look so bad in the eyes of those who have suffered "the slings and arrows of outrageous fortune." We try to make a case for the goodness of God to those who want to know how a loving God can allow such bad things to happen to so many good people.

When I was pastor of a small church, a great tragedy befell one of the families in my congregation. Their nine-year-old boy became the victim of leukemia. The cancer weakened him and reduced his once healthy body to skin and bones. Through months of suffering, the boys' parents and all of the church members prayed that God would exercise His power and make the boy well again. All-night prayer vigils were held. Other churches were asked to invite their congregations to join with ours to pray for healing. Over and over people "claimed the victory" and spoke with assurance that they would see the power of God at work and the boy healed. But the child died. After weeks of excruciating suffering, his emaciated body stopped working.

My congregation was severely disappointed and confused. The boy's father stopped coming to church. As his pastor I went to visit him to encourage him to return to the church worship services and fellowship. I said to him, "Ralph, you can't stop believing in God because He didn't answer your prayers." Ralph answered, "You don't understand. I didn't stop believing in God; I hate Him."

I was not prepared for that answer and didn't know what to say. Ralph figured that if God had the power to do something to help, and yet stood idly by while his little boy suffered untold agony, then God was cruel and he would hate Him for His cruelty.

Where Was God?

Another situation wherein sincere Christians believe God should
have acted but did not was the Holocaust in the Nazi concentra-
tion camps. Rabbi R.L. Rubenstein, a leading Jewish theologian, lived through the horror of seeing six million Jews gassed
and burned in prison incinerators. People prayed. They begged
God to use His power and stop the suffering. But nothing happened. As far as Rabbi Rubenstein was concerned, there could
be no higher purpose served through such an insane and perverted destruction of life. No redeeming results from such evil
and suffering could justify the nonintervention of God. There
was no way, to Rubenstein's thinking, that such events could
be made to serve some glorious plan. Six million Jews were
systematically put to death and God did nothing. Innocent children were destroyed. Bright and wonderful teenagers like Anne
Frank had their lives snuffed out. Helpless older people were
cruelly tortured and God did nothing. Rubenstein, like many
Jewish theologians since the Holocaust, concluded that God
must be dead. He must not exist. There could be no way
of believing in an omnipotent, loving God in the face of such
evil.

Recently, another Jewish rabbi wrote a best-seller entitled
When Bad Things Happen to Good People. His son was a victim
of a disease which caused rapid aging. He had to watch helpless-
ly as his dear boy grew old and died before the age of 12. As
a religious leader he knew all the "right" answers. He knew
that he was supposed to say that this tragedy was part of some
great plan of God and that through this suffering wonderful
blessings would be forthcoming. He knew that he was supposed
to believe that through this trial God was teaching him things
and helping him to grow. He knew all the pat answers to suffering
taught in theological seminaries. He had read the books. He had
heard the arguments, but none of them worked. All of then rang
hollow. None of the old answers brought him comfort.

After much thought he concluded that God wanted to help but could not, that God loved his boy but did not have the power to stop the suffering. Strangely, this answer did not upset him. Quite the opposite. He felt good about God. He concluded that it was better to have a God who cared but could not help, than to have a God who could help and did not care. He concluded that God was all-loving but not all-powerful.

A Limited God?

Certainly, I do not offer such an answer to the question of why good people suffer or why there is so much agony and evil in the world. Nor do I want to suggest that God could not stop it all from happening. What is more, I want to affirm that one day He *will* stop it all. Someday, perhaps sooner than we think, He will return and bring all things under His control. "For He must reign, until He has put all His enemies under His feet. The last enemy to be destroyed is death" (1 Corinthians 15:25–26).

However, between now and that hour when He returns to exercise His dominion over all the principalities and powers, His power is limited. The thing that we Christians want to make clear is that God has limited Himself—His limitation is self-imposed.

A limited God? A God that is not all powerful? A God who lacks omnipotence? Such ideas boggle the mind and reek of heresy. It has always been part of Christian orthodoxy to hold that God can do anything but fail. We evangelicals have hailed the Lord as the one who controls events and dictates the way things should be. And yet, it may be that our overemphasis on His omnipotence has dealt Him an injustice. It may be that by upholding His power, we have called His love into question. It may be that we ascribe to Him power that He does not want to use.

In the Book of Philippians is a message that we can read and reread without really grasping its implications:

> Let this mind be in you,
> which was also in Christ Jesus;
> who, being in the form of God,
> thought it not robbery to be equal with God;
> but made Himself of no reputation,
> and took upon Him the form of a servant,
> and was made in the likeness of men;
> and being found in fashion as a man,
> he humbled Himself,
> and became obedient unto death,
> even the death of the cross (Philippians 2:5–8, KJV).

Biblical scholars often refer to this passage as the *kenosis* passage because in the original Greek version of this portion of Scripture, the word *kenosis* is of crucial significance. The word means "to empty" and necessitates a radical interpretation of these verses, inviting us to a deeper understanding of the incarnation of Jesus.

In Jesus, God expressed Himself in a way that is shocking. He expressed Himself as a God of love and in the process set aside power. The story of the baby in Bethlehem's manger is meant to be much more than a sentimental story to elicit good feelings at Christmas time. That story expresses and demonstrates the way God has chosen to come to us.

In the birth of Jesus, God entered history as a vulnerable infant. On that first Christmas, Jehovah was incarnated in the weakness of a child. He would grow up like other children. He would have times when, like other children, He would be tired and need rest and sleep. He would have to study, ask questions, and learn from His elders. To the other children of Nazareth, He probably seemed to be very much like them. He lived among them with all the weaknesses of a growing child but with one difference—He was without sin. But He did not resist evil and live a pure life merely by depending upon Himself. Instead, it was in dependence on the Father that He found the wherewithal to conquer the temptations of the flesh. He was as weak as any of us, but He grew in fellowship with the Father and therein found strength to overcome the evil one.

When the leaders of Christendom were forced by historical circumstances to designate which of the many books written about Jesus should be included in the canon (the accepted books of the Bible), they found it necessary to reject some writings which had gained popularity among believers. In one of the rejected books, there is a description of the child Jesus playing with some of the boys of Nazareth. A few of them are mean to Jesus and treat Him with great cruelty. In the story Jesus responds by raising His hand to these children and striking them dead. In another story, Jesus is playing in the mud with some of His friends. He and the others set themselves to the task of making models of animals out of the clay. Jesus makes some clay birds, and in this fanciful story He finishes off His project by snapping His fingers so that the birds come to life and fly away.

These writings were never included in Scripture for obvious reasons. The stores are totally out of character with the nature of our Lord. God did not incarnate Himself as a superboy who dazzled His peers with magic tricks. The church fathers knew that Jesus grew up as one of us, taking on our frailties and weaknesses. They knew that in Jesus, God had abandoned His power and majesty in order to present Himself as one whom we could imitate. If it had been otherwise, He would not have been able to ask us to be like Him.

A friend of mine who often speaks to students at Christian colleges regularly asks the question, "Did Jesus understand radar?" In many cases the students answer, "Yes!" They fail to recognize that if Jesus, living 2,000 years ago, had understood a twentieth-century invention, He would not have been a normal human being. The Incarnation would have been a put-on. His humanity would have been a pretense. Such was not the case. He really was born as one of us.

Gnosticism

It is interesting to note that among the liberal theologians of our day there are those who doubt the divinity of Christ. Many scholarly writers refuse to believe that Jesus was a full and complete incarnation of God. This contemporary heresy is just the opposite of the most common hersey expressed in the life and times of the early church, which was to doubt the humanity of Jesus. The ancient heretics found it inconceivable and totally unbelievable that God should take on the nature of man. One group of heretics called the Gnostics claimed that Jesus only appeared to have a human body; in reality He was an omnipotent, spiritual presence pretending to be a man. So pervasive was this heresy among the early Christians that John had to make a special emphasis of the humanity of Jesus when he wrote in his Gospel: "And the Word was made flesh, and dwelt among us, (and we beheld His glory, the glory as of the only begotten of the Father) full of grace and truth" (John 1:14, KJV). Christians living in a Hellenistic culture found it difficult to believe that God could be reduced to the frail condition of being in the flesh like the rest of us.

I sometimes think that many evangelical Christians tend toward being modern counterparts of the ancient Gnostics. While our theologically liberal opponents doubt the deity of Jesus, we have a tendency to diminish His humanity. We find it disconcerting and uncomfortable to view Jesus as fully human. We want to perpetuate the belief that He was different from the rest of us in that He had powers and knowledge which were transhuman. We refuse to grasp the fact that He *learned* the Scriptures, *grew* into spiritual maturity, and performed no mighty works in His own power.

God entered human history in order to bring men and women into His kingdom through His love. He chose to redeem humanity and transform society through sacrificial self-giving, rather than through awesome demonstrations of power. It is in the context of this reality that the temptation of Jesus by Satan becomes pertinent for our discussion. In Luke 4 we read that Jesus ended His 40 days of fasting in the wilderness by confronting the wiles of the devil. The Lord was tempted to use His power to attract followers. "Change stones into bread. . . . Float down to ground safely after You jump from the pinnacle of the temple. . . . Dazzle the people with power," the evil one suggests. "Then You will have them in the palm of Your hand." But Jesus knew that by yielding to the use of power as the instrument for salvation, He would be bowing to Satan and worshiping the ways of the demonic.

Jesus really did abandon power when He lived among us. He wasn't simply holding back and pretending to possess our physical limitations—He truly was one of us. We don't like that fact and do our best to suppress it. We want to think of Him disguising Himself as a sophisticated Rotarian who could step into a phone booth, rip off His robes, and show us who He is—a first-century Clark Kent/Superman.

Judas was one who refused to accept such a limited Messiah. On Palm Sunday, power had been within the Master's grasp. It was the logical time to take over. It was the opportunity to rally the masses to the cause, the hour when He should claim power. And Jesus let it all slip away.

Some think that Judas betrayed Jesus in order to force Him to play the power game and establish His rule. Those who hold this theory suggest that Judas felt that if Jesus were left with no alternature, He would be forced away from His reluctance to seize the throne. If that was the plan of Judas, it all backfired. Perhaps it was when he realized that his attempt to manipulate Jesus into using power only resulted in the death of one who had loved Him infinitely that Judas hanged himself.

Jesus really became one of us. There were no magic tricks up His sleeves. When mighty works were done through Him, he humbly admitted that He was not the one who deserved the credit. The glory belonged to the Father.

What Can God Do?

In time of trouble, we all want a God who will appear like a genie and magically make things right. We expect a sophisticated masculine version of Mary Poppins to come floating into our lives just when we need Him and take care of all the obnoxious details and difficulties.

What good can come from a God who empties Himself of power? What can such a God offer us? How does He think He can get us to follow Him, if He doesn't destroy our enemies and establish the only kind of kingdom that people can understand?

Recently, I was the speaker at a program marking the end of a training program for inmates in some of the largest prisons in this country. They had come to know Christ while they were in prison and had been released for a three-week period to prepare themselves to witness to their fellow inmates and serve as evangelists within the prison system. This gathering was to mark the end of their preparation time. There was a certain sadness in the meeting because these men knew that the next day they would be back in jail cells.

I had sat with them for several hours, listening to their stories. The agonies that marked their lives were almost too difficult for them to share. One man had raped and murdered a ten-year-old girl. His family had disowned him, and his children hated him. He had not received a card or a letter from any family member for years.

Another man told me that his mother was dying of cancer, but that he was unable to be with her in her last days.

Still another shared with me the fact that his wife had given up on him and had taken up with another man, and his children had been taught to call this new mate Father. It was hard for me to hold back the tears as I listened to them.

Just before I had my opportunity to speak to the group, a guest soloist was introduced. She said that before she sang she wanted to share a testimony with the group. "On the way here

I was driving in my brand new Ford. Unfortunately, I was right behind a large dump truck filled with stones. One of the stones fell off the truck, hit the road, and bounced up onto my car. It nicked my windshield and I was very depressed. When I got out of the car I looked at the nick on that windshield and I said, 'Lord, You know how unhappy that nick is making me.' So I put my finger on the nick and prayed that Jesus would heal it. And would you believe that He did?"

The prisoner sitting next to me at the meeting mumbled, "No!" No wonder so many people don't believe in God. When we finish describing Him, He is so unattractive that they do not want to believe in Him. It is unbelievable that the loving God revealed in Jesus should turn a deaf ear to the passionate pleas of a pervert and the agonized cries of a repentent son in prison but zip right down and heal a nicked windshield, if the one praying uses just the right words.

After the meeting the soloist told me that the men didn't get their prayers answered because they didn't end them with the verbal formula, "In Jesus name." She actually believed that the God of glory could be manipulated into performing magic tricks on our behalf if we just employed the right incantation. In my opinion, the naive beliefs of primitive religions with witch doctors are deserving of more respect.

What Does God Offer?

I know what you're thinking because I have the same tendency. If God cannot be depended upon to get rid of the dents in my fenders, pay my bills, or help me find parking places, then what *can* I expect Him to do? In a far more serious vein, if praying to God won't automatically cure my mother's cancer, result in my child's salvation, or keep my friend from being killed in Vietnam, what *does* He offer me?

The answer is *love*. He offers you love—the empathy of love, the concern of love, the fellowship of love, the sharing of love.

When you hurt, you can expect Jesus to hurt with you. When your heart is broken and the pain is unbearable, you can know that His heart is broken with yours. When in agony you cry, "My God, my God, why hast Thou forsaken me?" He answers, "I know your agony; I understand your sense of aloneness; I am with you."

He weeps with those who weep and suffers with those who suffer. Lovers always do. Love suffers long and is kind. Love patiently endures all things, bears all things, and believes all things (1 Corinthians 13:5–7). Perfect love casts out all fears (1 John 4:18). Love covers a multitude of sins (1 Peter 4:8). Love never fails, even when everything else does. And when everything else has passed away, love remains (1 Corinthians 13:8). God is love and love is what He offers you.

While on a speaking tour in England, I was asked to address a group of people in a community noted for its intellectuals. The person who had set up the meeting told me that some prominent peace movement leaders and Marxist intellectuals would be present. My address was supposed to be one that would make Christianity credible to those who had sophisticated commitments to the social sciences.

At the conclusion of the meeting, I invited anyone who wanted to talk further about Jesus to remain because I would make myself available for discussion. One very bright woman stayed and talked with me. I expected that she would try to show the flaws in my presentation and critique my remarks from a Marxist perspective. She had the style and vocabulary of many of the intellectuals I have met on campuses around the world. We talked for a brief period and then I asked her quite simply, "Why can't you believe in God?"

She stopped talking and after a long pause I noticed that tears were beginning to appear in her eyes. She said, "I have never been married, but I have been pregnant. I wanted to have the baby more than anything else I have ever wanted. When the child was born, he was the victim of spinal meningitis and soon was dead. I couldn't believe that a loving God would allow such a thing to happen. If He loved me and loved the child, and if He had the power to save the child's life, why didn't He?"

I said to her, "The God who was revealed in Jesus Christ offers you His love, not His power. He did not save your child, not because He didn't want to, but because He chooses to be in our world in the weakness of His love rather than in the strength of His power. However, I do know that if you cry, He cries with you. As your heart is broken, His is broken too. Whatever agony you experience, His is far more. As much as you love that baby, Jesus loves him more. I do not offer you a theological explanation as to why this terrible thing happened. Instead, I offer you a Jesus who shares your sorrows and your pains. I offer you a Jesus who wants to bear your burden if you will let Him. I invite you to accept a Jesus who comes not in power but with a broken heart. Will you accept Him?"

She did, for she was enticed not by the power of God, but by the God who presents Himself as a suffering servant in Jesus Christ.

An Offer of Love

Futuristic novelists have looked into the future describing a world created by science which is problem-free. Aldous Huxley's *Brave New World* and George Orwell's *1984* both offer a future world in which there will be no more sorrow and suffering. But it is also a world in which there will be no more love.

If God had come to us in power, we would have bent our knees before Him in submission. We would be reduced to nothing before Him. We would be groveling before His throne and trembling in His presence. But the good news is that He comes to us in love and invites us to be His friends (John 15:14–15). Prayer is not a time to fearfully stand before some transcendental shylock who demands his pound of flesh. Instead it is a time of intimate fellowship with a lover.

When Jesus taught us how to pray, He told us to address God as "Our Father" (Matthew 6:9). This word for father is the Hebrew word *Abba,* which is roughly akin to our word "daddy." The Apostle Paul made the same point in his Epistle to the Romans: "For you did not receive a spirit that makes you a slave again to fear; but you received the Spirit of Sonship. And by Him we cry, '*Abba,* Father' " (Romans 8:15).

To the ancient Hebrews, the suggestion that Jehovah be addressed as Daddy must have seemed close to blasphemy. Indeed, the idea may have the same effect on many contemporary church people who have been trained to talk to God as to a majestic potentate. I personally appreciate the formalized petitioning of the Almighty which marks many Christian worship services. I was trained to use the proper ascriptions in prayer and thusly say,

> O Thou, the great Creator of the universe,
> O Thou who doth feed me, clothe me,
> and provide me with every good and perfect gift,
> I beseech Thee this day to be present with me. . . .

However, I cannot imagine my 19-year-old son walking into the house and saying to me:

> O thou chairman of the Sociology Department
> at Eastern College,
> O thou who doth clothe me, feed me,
> and provide me with every good and perfect gift,
> I beseech thee this day—lend me the car!

He doesn't talk to me that way for a very simple reason—I am his dad and we are intimate. He hugs me, he kisses me, and he talks to me as a son talks to his dad.

God has chosen to be closer to each of us than anyone else can be. He wants us to have an intimate personal relationship to Him that allows us to enter into Him and He into each of us. Many people who believe in Jesus have never come to know God that way. They have not grasped the wonder and ecstasy of being personally loved by God. They are impressed by His creative power, but they do not know that He lays aside the garments of His station and humbly presents Himself in love.

Some may want the awesome potentate whose countenance is too glorious to behold, whose ark demolishes any who would get close enough to touch. For me, the good news is that the great One who is totally other and past finding out has humbled Himself and presented Himself to us not in power but in love. He is waiting to be confronted on a cross. Weak and frail, suffering and battered, He invites each of us to love Him as the crucified One, the One who has demonstrated His love for us by laying down His life for us. "Greater love has no one than this, that one lay down his life for his friends" (John 15:13).

The God of creation who manifested Himself in Jesus is available to anyone who will surrender to His love. The Apostle Paul did not have a relationship with God marked by distance and restraint. His desire was:

> I want to know Christ, and the power of His resurrection, and the fellowship of sharing in His sufferings, becoming like Him in His death (Philippians 3:10).

Drawing Power

Please do not misunderstand me. I am not saying that God has no power to perform miracles, or that the testimonies of godly people who tell how God intervened in their lives during times of trouble are simply illusions. God is God and He can do what He wants when He wants. What I want to affirm is what the Bible tells us—the good news that God has chosen to set aside His power in His efforts to win us to Himself. He does not seek to overawe us with wonders and miracles, but rather seeks to draw us to Him by revealing Himself as a sacrificial lover. In Christ He says: "But I, when I am lifted up from the earth, will draw all men to Myself" (John 12:32).

We are drawn to a God who presents Himself to us not as one who can put the stars in space and set the earth spinning on its axis, but as a broken man nailed spread-eagle to a Roman cross outside a city wall.

We would be dazzled if He came to us in awesome splendor. But we can love Him only as He comes to us in the frailty of the flesh. At the cross I love Him. As I close my eyes and see Him riveted there with spikes through His wrists and feet, with the spear wound in His side, I want to cry for Him and pity Him. When I visualize the crown of thorns tearing His skin and the blood and sweat running down over His contorted face, I want to reach up and wipe His brow. As I listen to the cries from His parched throat, I want to press a cup of cool water to His lips. He seems so tired and frail that I wish I could have carried His cross for Him. And then I hear Him say, "You can! You can carry My cross. Those who reach out to help Me can be part of My kingdom."

It is only upon reflection that I realize that this weak and suffering Man is my Lord and my God. I find myself loving Him only as I forget about His power.

9
When All Else Fails

What Happens When
Power Must Be Used

I have so emphasized the love of God that it might sound as if God does not use His power at all. While God choses to set aside power when He attempts to establish love relationships with us, He has awesome power to use when He wills to do so. He is the Almighty One, a God whose power is so great that none can stand against Him and win. He is a God who speaks and His words create a universe out of nothing; a God who can make the armies of earth come to naught, who can annihilate the world at a stroke. My claim is not that God does not have power; rather, that in order to express His love, He emptied Himself of power and presented Himself to us as a man on a cross.

Power is used by God, but not for redemptive purposes. He redeems, renews, and heals through His love. He uses power to destroy what will not be saved and to consume what threatens those He loves. To use words which some modern sophisticates might deem medieval, but which are nevertheless biblical and true, He uses His power to destroy the works of the devil (1 John 3:8).

His power must be exercised in our individual lives if we are to be freed from those destructive tendencies and qualities which prevent us from realizing our new humanity as evidenced in Christ. Each of us needs to be purged from the lusts of the flesh and the will to power which are all too evident in our lives. I often find myself unable to control or suppress the demonic tendencies which are evident in my personality.

For instance, sexual lust is very much a part of my make-up. It threatens to overwhelm me and I find that my own willpower is not sufficient to combat it. At such times I can call upon God to suppress the lust with His power. He can control and destroy what must be controlled and destroyed if I am to live in accord with His will. He can do in me what I cannot do for myself.

One day I was talking with a group of men at a Christian businessmen's luncheon about the struggles I have in my battle against lust. I shared with them in honesty and told them about the ways I am tempted intensely and regularly to yield to sexual gratifications that would destroy me. After the meeting one of the men came up to me and said he was shocked that such a person was allowed to be the speaker at a Christian gathering. He went on to explain that since he was "saved" these kinds of things never happened to him and that he seriously doubted if I was really a Christian. I resisted the urge to call him a liar, and tried to explain to him that temptation is not sin. It is yielding to temptation and deciding to do what the lust of the flesh entices us to do that constitutes sin. But he would not buy my explanation. Undoubtedly, he was one of those "holier-than-thou" hypocrites who pretended to be shocked when Jimmy Carter confessed to a magazine reporter that he often had problems with lust.

Fortunately, Jesus understands what I am talking about. What is more, He has been through the same temptations. The Bible says that He was tempted in all the ways that we are tempted and yet was without sin (Hebrews 4:15). Satan worked on Jesus more than any other man in history. If the evil one could have gotten Jesus to yield to temptation, he would have conquered all of us in one coup.

Jesus experienced all the temptations that we do, but with even greater intensity, and He knew how to conquer them. He leaned on His Father. He did not trust in His own strength but in the strength of the One who had sent Him into the world. His way is the only way we can have victories over temptations. By asking God to win the battles with the flesh, we can be "more than conquerers" (Romans 8:37). God's power is sufficient to provide us with victory in our struggles with the demonic forces which constantly attack us.

The Apostle Paul told of his struggles with the evil tendencies of the flesh:

> For the good that I would, I do not; but the evil which I would not, that I do. Now if I do that I would not, it is no more I that do it, but sin that dwelleth in me. I find then a law, that, when I would do good, evil is present with me. For I delight in the law of God after the inward man; but I see another law in my members, warring against the law of my mind, and bringing me into captivity to the law of sin which is in my members. O wretched man that I am! Who shall deliver me from the body of this death? (Romans 7:19–24, KJV)

Paul found comfort in the power of God which made him able to survive temptations.

> I thank God through Jesus Christ our Lord. So then with the mind I myself serve the law of God; but with the flesh the law of sin (Romans 7:25, KJV).

Gluttony

One of the most common but seldom discussed temptations is the tendency to overeat. The sin of overeating is even more apparent within a world inhabited by five hundred million malnourished and hungry people. Everywhere I go, I see people who are far too fat for their own good and the good of their Christian testimony. We make light of the sin of overeating, as though it were simply a bad habit and not an abomination in the eyes of God.

In spite of our tendency to treat lightly the sin of overeating, the medieval preachers listed it among the seven deadly sins. We react by thinking that such a judgment is a bit too severe. Oh, we quite readily admit that it isn't a nice thing to do, but we are reluctant to list it among the "Big Seven." Nevertheless, obesity was taken seriously by the preachers of the Middle Ages, in large measure because it was taken seriously by the biblical prophets. Amos condemned people who became as "fat as cows" while there were people around them who were starving:

> Hear this word, ye kine of Bashan that are in the mountain of Samaria, which oppress the poor, which crush the needy, which say to their masters, "Bring, and let us drink." The Lord God hath sworn by His holiness, that, lo, the days shall come upon you, that He will take you away with hooks, and your posterity with fishhooks. And ye shall go out at the breaches, every cow at that which is before her; and ye shall cast them into the palace, saith the Lord (Amos 4:1–3, KJV).

Overeating is not only harmful to the body, which is called the temple of the Lord; but it is insensitive to the needs of the underfed peoples of Third World countries. How could those whose children starve believe that we love them when they know we overeat? Incidentally, the man who tore me up for my confession over feelings of lust was fantastically overweight.

People tell me they try to diet but just don't have the willpower to fight the desire to overeat. Well, the good news of the Gospel is that God has the power to enable them to overcome this temptation. Furthermore, their obesity is evidence that they have yielded to the demonic and have refused to allow God to empower them to suppress the desires of the flesh. I am amazed at how many ministers take to the pulpit with their stomachs hanging over their belts, not realizing that they are displaying the evidence of sin in their lives, even as they call their hearers to repentance for other sins.

Oral Roberts was severly criticized when he instituted a program at his university to end obesity among his students. He required that all who matriculated at his school who were overweight would have to go on a diet and enter into a special program of exercising until they had their weight under control.

Many of those who criticized Roberts thought his policy was for cosmetic purposes—that he did not want unattractive people on his campus. Such critics missed the point. Oral Roberts was justifiably concerned about the tendency toward gluttony which is all too evident among Christians.

For those who are tempted to overeat, there is good news that God can provide the power to gain victory in this area of life. Those with tendencies to overeat must learn to pray to God who can supply the power to control the appetites. This is no small thing for Christians to consider. I know it will upset many fat people to realize that obesity may be as serious as adultery and that those who overeat "crucify Christ anew." Well, they should be upset. They should be so upset that they repent and ask God to provide the power to conquer the temptation to gluttony.

God wants to eliminate in us what cannot be redeemed by His love. Anything that would keep us from growing into the fullness of the stature of Christ must be rooted out and destroyed. That is why Jesus said:

> I tell you that anyone who looks at a woman lustfully has already committed adultery with her in his heart. If your right eye causes

you to sin, gouge it out and throw it away. It is better for you to lose one part of your body than for your whole body to be thrown into hell. And if your right hand causes you to sin, cut it off and throw it away. It is better for you to lose one part of your body than for your whole body to go into hell (Matthew 5:28–30).

God only accepts what is pure and that is why He wishes to purge us of all impurities. Paul wrote:

Every man's work shall be made manifest; for the day shall declare it, because it shall be revealed by fire; and the fire shall try every man's work of what sort it is. If any man's work abide which he hath built thereupon, he shall receive a reward. If any man's work shall be burned, he shall suffer loss; but he himself shall be saved; yet so as by fire (1 Corinthians 3:13–15, KJV).

God uses His power to destroy what must be destroyed even as He uses His love to redeem what can be redeemed. Thus, while His power is terrible, we must welcome its painful work in our lives.

Christian Forgetting

God works in our lives in yet another way, as He purges us from the memory of those things which must be forgotten if we are to live in joy. As wonderful as His forgiveness of sin is, we have this added wonder of learning that He is a God who forgets. Our sins are blotted out, buried in the deepest sea, remembered no more. God not only forgives but He forgets.

It would be terrible to go to heaven if He did not forget. I cannot imagine what it would be like to approach the throne of God and have Him say, "Campolo! We've been waiting for you. Peter, get the Campolo Book!" I can just hear Peter answering, "Book? We've got a library on this guy, Lord!"

I do not know if there is a Campolo Book in heaven. But if

there is, only good things will be written in it. You ask, "What about all the bad stuff in your life? What about all the filth and rottenness?" I can answer with excitement, "It's all blotted out! None of it is remembered!"

What God has done for us we must do for others. We must forget the evil they have done. To do otherwise is to offer something less than Christian forgiveness. Not to forget what should be forgotten is to be possessed by a spiritual cancer that can destroy our religious health and sap the joy from our living.

One evening I preached in a small church in Indiana. Following the service a young couple came to talk with me. They were about to end their marriage, but the wife thought that through counseling they might find a way to save it. I sat down with them in a small room behind the sanctuary. As I listened to their story, I found that the basis of their difficulty lay in the young man's desire for adulterous relationships. The stories of his many affairs were brought out and the details were lurid and offensive. At first he was arrogant about it all and seemed almost amused. However, just as I was about to give up on him, the Holy Spirit began to work in him. The young man broke and his arrogance turned to humility. His smirk turned to tears. He repented and accepted Jesus as his personal Saviour. He begged for another chance and I assured him he could have one because our God is a God of second chances. We prayed together, and as the couple left that little room, I was absolutely convinced that they were on their way to marital bliss.

Two years later I was back in their part of the country on another speaking engagement. After I finished delivering my address, they once again asked to see me. This time I was thrilled to have the opportunity to talk with them. I assumed that the husband's new life in Christ had ushered in a satisfying marital lifestyle. I thought they had come to thank me for counseling them two years earlier and I was preparing myself for some compliments. When I asked how things were going, he said, "It's been hell."

"I thought you became a Christian the last time we were together. I thought your life would be changed and your marital problems solved."

"I did become a Christian," he said. "My life has been changed. I've tried to be a good husband and have been completely faithful to my wife."

"It's me," the young wife interjected. "It's me! I can't forget what he's done. I can't forget those other women. Every time he tries to touch me, I think where those hands have been and what they have done, and I cringe."

I said, "You must forget. You must not only forgive; you must forget."

"I can't," she said.

"I know," I responded. "But I believe that God has the power to destroy the memory of what has gone before. I believe that the Holy Spirit can purge your mind of the hurt and pain of the past. I believe that God can root out of your consciousness what keeps you from love. Why not ask the Lord to use His power to destroy the memory of those ugly things which torture you?"

We prayed and I am waiting to learn if she allowed the Lord to destroy the works of the devil in her life.

Are we not all in need of purging by the power of God? Do we not all need to have the memory of many things wiped from our consciousness? Do we not all realize that the memory of past hurts inflicted on us must be removed, like ugly tumors must be removed from the body? Well, the good news is that God has the power to bring about destruction of the ugliness of our yesterdays, freeing us to love today.

When Parents Must Use Power

When I was a boy, and my father punished me, he said what many fathers say to their children, "This is going to hurt me more than it will hurt you." As he paddled my rear end, I found that very hard to believe. Time has passed; now I am a father and on several occasions I have had to punish my son. I can assure you that my father was right. Punishing children must be the most difficult part of parenting and yet at times it becomes necessary.

Parents want their children to voluntarily do what is good. They do not want to force their children to be obedient. They want their children to do what is right because they are motivated by love and reason rather than by threats of punishment. Whenever a child is punished, particularly when that punishment is corporal in nature, the parents experience a sense of failure. They inwardly say, "If we had raised our child better, this would not be necessary." Or, "If my child loved me more, he would obey me better."

The parents of one teenager who was arrested on a drug use charge could only say, over and over again, "How could he do this after we loved him so much?" They viewed their son's wrong behavior as evidence of his not responding to their love. They had found a large supply of marijuana cigarettes in his room and also discovered a significant quantity of cocaine. Upon investigation they learned that he was selling drugs to his friends to earn money to pay for his own drug habit. When they realized what had happened in their son's life, they decided to turn him over to the police. It was with deep regret that they resorted to the use of force to correct their son. As they did so, there was a tremendous sense of failure on their part. Nevertheless, they knew that punishment was necessary and that they had to try to force their son to do what was right.

Children are tempted to establish themselves as adults by seeking power. They want to be in charge of their lives. They want to be able to decide for themselves what they will do and when they will do it. They do not want other people, especially their parents, telling them what they can and cannot do. Consequently, children often defy their parents, testing them, to see what they can get away with.

Sometimes the parents yield to the claims for independence and power only to find that the children are not happy with the power they have gained. This is because children are somewhat ambivalent about power.

On the one hand, they are tempted to secure it. If they are not checked, they will tend to dominate their parents. We have all witnessed situations in which children have gained control over their parents.

On the other hand, children usually feel insecure when they are able to dominate their parents. They lack confidence and are afraid of being in charge. They realize that their freedom from the directions of their parents leaves them with the burden of deciding for themselves what is best and what will make them happy, and they are not sure that they are up to deciding properly. In such situations, children are relieved when the parents reestablish their control, even if the means is punishment.

I remember times when my children in their early years tried to assert themselves and take charge of their lives. They would do this by trying to defy my wishes and the wishes of my wife. They would refuse to do what they were told. My wife, who was the more compassionate of the two of us, would endeavor to reason with them and show them through careful explanations why it would be best for them to do what they were told. These discussions would go on and on, with the children becoming more and more agitated.

The mistake was to think that the children were simply confused and needed clarification, that all that was necessary was to show them that their parents' way was best for them. The talking never worked. In the end they had to be punished. Sometimes that punishment would take the form of a paddling. Much to our surprise and relief, the children usually calmed down immediately upon being punished. They actually seemed happier and, in reality, they were. By exercising power over them, we had taken control of them. They knew they were no longer in charge and they were greatly relieved to relinquish the power that was more than they could handle. We never enjoyed punishing our children but we found it necessary. We wished that they would be obedient out of love; but in the absence of loving obedience, we had to use force to bring them under control.

Every child will press to determine the limits of his power. If no limits are set, the child will press farther and farther until he is deemed uncontrollable. The child must be stopped from pursuing such a self-destructive course. Unfortunately, this can only be done by the parents forcing their will on the child. This is never happy for the parents, but they know it must be done. Power is essential when love does not work.

Sometimes parents come to me for counsel and ask, "If my child does not want to go to church, should I make him?" They usually go on to say, "I'm afraid that if I force him to go, he will end up hating church and never go again." What these parents need to realize is that the child may not so much be rebelling against church as he is rebelling against them. He may be testing their willingness to stand up to his demands and may be exploring the extent of his powers. The problem may have nothing to do with church, but may be a test of the parents' resolve to get him to obey them. In such a case, to yield to the child's demands is to encourage him to further challenge their authority.

Every child is born with the same will to power that has marked humanity from the time of Adam. Each one seeks to have his own way. Consequently, there is a rebellious spirit evident among growing children and that rebellious spirit must be challenged by the power of the parents.

10
The Need for Good People in a Bad World

What Christians Should Do About Politics

Few things generate more controversy among Christians than politics. Nevertheless, it is essential that our discussion of power give consideration to the question of how Christians can participate in government.

Some have suggested that followers of Jesus should stay out of public office because the possession of power will corrupt them. In 1976, when I was a candidate for the United States Congress, many of my Christian friends told me that I had no business getting involved in politics because it would ruin my testimony. They were convinced that no one could hold a powerful public position without being sucked into a sinful lifestyle. "After all," they pointed out, "isn't politics the art of compromising?"

I have many close associates and friends who are Mennonites and others who are members of the Church of the Brethren. These wonderful Christians out of the Anabaptist tradition believe that Christians should stay out of public office because it is not proper for disciples of Jesus to use the force of the state to coerce people into compliance with what is right. They believe that we should invite people to do God's will and hope that compliance will be brought about through the loving persuasion of Christians.

The Mennonites believe that Christians should stay out of all positions which would necessitate forcing people to obey the principles of love and justice. Consequently, they ask the members of their churches to refuse to serve in the military or as policemen, to stay out of labor unions, and not hold public office.

The Power Dilemma

While the views of my Mennonite friends are very attractive, I am reminded again of Edmund Burke's important statement: "All that is necessary for the forces of evil to win in the world is for enough good men to do nothing." It is obvious that if Christians stay out of positions of power, such positions may be filled by persons whose values and behavior could be anti-Christian and detrimental to the well-being of society. While power frightens me, I am aware of what happens when Christians abandon power to the ruthless and corrupt.

Leo Tolstoy, the brilliant Russian novelist who wrote *War and Peace,* sought to live out the Christian life as set forth in the Sermon on the Mount. He believed that only simple compliance with the teachings of Jesus could provide him with inner peace and assurance of salvation. For him, this meant selling everything he owned and giving all his money away to the poor.

He was master of a huge estate that employed scores of workers. The peasants who lived and worked on his land enjoyed the benefits of his benevolent and just spirit. Tolstoy cared for the needs of his servants and provided them with decent housing and adequate food.

When he sold his estate, it fell into the hands of ruthless owners who beat the workers when they did not work at the required speed. They exploited the laborers and failed to supply them with needed food.

The workers cried out for help, appealing to Tolstoy to deliver them from their sufferings. But he was no longer in a position where he could help. He had abandoned power in order to be more Christian and his decision had led to intense suffering for others.

One contemporary philosopher has properly argued that Christians are caught in the dilema in which they are required to take positions of power, even though it is impossible to exercise power without limiting the ability to express love.

Powers Are of God

Those in the Reformed tradition, the Presbyterians, Baptists, Congregationalists, and Reformed churches, have taken a more positive view toward participation in government. They point out that the Bible teaches that government is ordained of God. In Colossians 1:16 we read that political systems were created by God:

> For by Him all things were created; things in heaven, and on earth, visible and invisible, whether thrones or powers or rulers or authorities; all things were created by Him and for Him.

Whatever the process by which they emerged in society, the Apostle Paul makes it clear that governments are willed to exist by God. Evil must be restrained, order must be preserved, and society must be protected from its deviant elements. Political power exists to suppress the destruction that results when sinful people give vent to their lusts and passions. When our behavior is governed by the love of God, there is no need to fear the rule of just government. Love leads to compliance with the law.

> For rulers hold no terror for those who do right, but for those who do wrong. Do you want to be free from fear of the one in authority? Then do what is right and he will commend you. For

he is God's servant to do you good. But if you do wrong, be afraid, for he does not bear the sword for nothing. He is God's servant, an agent of wrath to bring punishment on the wrongdoer. Love does no harm to its neighbor. Therefore, love is the fulfillment of the law (Romans 13:3–4, 10).

Many consider Romans 13 to be the most crucial chapter in the Bible dealing with the role of government. In this chapter, we see that the role of government is not redemptive but rather for the purpose of controlling and destroying evil. This relates to what I said about God using love for creation and redemption, and power for destroying what cannot be saved.

Power Abusers

Christians have always been suspicious of those who hold power because they are well aware of the sinful tendencies inherent in all human beings since the fall of Adam. They know all too well that people in power often lose their self-restraint and use their power to provide personal gratification.

David, the best of the kings of Israel, raised havoc for his nation because he had the power to do what he pleased. One day, while his nation was at war, King David was on the balcony of his palace when his eyes fell upon Bathsheba, a beautiful woman who was the wife of Uriah, a soldier who was away serving Israel in battle. David burned with sexual desire as he saw her washing herself. Because he was the absolute monarch in Israel, he could do what he pleased without restraint; and he decided to gratify his sensual appetites and have sexual relations with Bathsheba.

Her ensuing pregnancy only enhanced the devious intrigue of David. He called Uriah back from the battle lines and tried to induce him to enjoy sexual pleasures with his wife so that the pregnancy might be attributed to him. As a faithful soldier, Uriah would not engage in sexual pleasures as long as his comrades were risking their lives in battle. Then the scheming of David became more sinister; he contrived a plan whereby he sent Uriah back into battle and gave instructions that he should be placed in the thick of the fighting where he was certain to be killed. As this evil plot is unfolded in Scripture, it shows that power can be extremely dangerous, even in the hands of a good man (2 Samuel 11).

Down through history the story has been the same, often with even more disastrous results. The chronicles of history are littered with stories of people who sought power with the promise that once they secured it, they would use it for the good of all. In case after case, the realization of power resulted in tyranny and oppression. We have all watched the succession of revolts and coups in unstable Third World nations. We have listened to the rhetoric of those who challenge established totalitarian regimes. We have heard the leaders of the "liberation" movements promise a new era of peace and freedom once the present government is ousted. Then, sadly, we have watched the new regime demonstrate even greater excesses of tyranny and oppression than the one which preceded it.

Power changes people, and even the best-intentioned are perverted by it. Frederick Nietzsche said, "Be careful when you fight a dragon, lest you become a dragon." Those who have sought to eliminate abusive political powers by the use of power usually become like the abusive system they challenge.

For that reason, Christians have tended to be politically conservative. From the perspective of sociology, conservatives are people who are suspicous of the power of government. Conservatives do not believe that government can do as much good as liberals believe it can do. They are not convinced by the rhetoric of even the most well-meaning aspirants to political office who claim that they can make the world a better place if they just have the power to do so. Conservatives realize that no human being can be trusted with power, because power allows the possessor to express his inherent diabolical tendencies.

In the mid-seventeenth century, when Puritan Christians gained control of England, that nation was subject to a totalitarian dictatorship that stifled the human spirit and elicited resentment toward God. Oliver Cromwell's rule of England leaves no one with an assurance that a nation will be healthy and good, if only "godly" rulers are in office.

The government of the United States was formed by conservatives who believed that those who have power cannot be trusted with it. That is why the Constitution contains a system of checks and balances. The President cannot do much without the consent of Congress, and the actions of Congress can be vetoed by the President. Furthermore, both Congress and the President can be restrained by decisions of the Supreme Court. The founders of this nation had learned much from the abuses of European monarchs and were determined not to allow themselves to fall under the control of any absolute ruler, no matter how good his intentions.

Cultural Imperative

Because of what political power does to people who possess it, contemporary Reformed theologians have encouraged Christians to enter politics and have called upon Christian citizens to exercise checks and controls over those who are in public office. Acting from John Calvin's "cultural imperative," Reformed Christians believe that God wills for them to invade every sector of their society and culture and endeavor to bring all things under the Lordship of Christ. To them this means that Christians must enter the political arena with the explicit purpose of transforming government into the kind of system that God wills for it to be. They also believe that Christians must never relinquish the right and the power to serve as a conscience to those who are in positions of power.

However, there is a big difference between being the conscience of the state and trying to control the state. I believe that it is this distinction which the Moral Majority has confused. Because its primary spokesman is a pastor who articulates his views from a pulpit, and on national television, the Moral Majority appears to be the church. Therefore, when it endeavors to control national policy, it seems to be doing something that the institutional church has no business doing.

There is no excuse for Christians to be politically ignorant or indifferent, or to say, "I'm not concerned with politics because I am dedicated to spiritual things." "All the world belongs to the Lord," claim those in the Reformed tradition. This means that there is no sector of society which can be excluded from the concerns of Christians.

Limits of Government

Even as Christians become involved with political concerns, they need to be constantly reminded of what government can and cannot do. It can restrain evil, and for this purpose it was ordained of God. However, we should not expect government to accomplish that good which flows from love. Government is an institution of power and can accomplish only what power can do, and that is to restrain and destroy evil.

The church is the body that God has called to do His work of love. There is no question but that the church should reach out to serve the poor and needy, instead of expecting the government to do so. The church has the financial means and the personnel to reach out to every suffering member of society. If every five church members would assume responsibility for one person on the welfare rolls, we could eliminate the need for public assistance to the poor. Undoubtedly, this is an unrealistic expectation; and the fact that it is shows that the church is unwilling to follow the Suffering Servant who is Jesus.

The Christian college where I teach has many students who

are committed to serving the needs of poor and oppressed peoples. Over the past few years they have begun to reach out into the nearby city and develop programs which usually are provided by the government. In one low-cost housing development, these young people have taken over many of the social services previously carried out by the city government. They have run summer day camps, established a variety of social clubs for teenagers, initiated job placement programs for adults, developed a tenant council which encourages community members to make those decisions which determine their social destiny, provided counseling and juvenile protection services for delinquent youth, and developed an array of evangelistic programs that are reaching the people of the community with the message of Jesus. The community has come alive. Redemptive work is being done. The people of God are doing the work of the church and the role of the city government in this community has diminished. The church is expressing the love of God through involvement in social programs, leaving the government to perform its role of restraining crime.

The withdrawal of evangelical Christians from social programs for almost a half century has been one of the contributing factors in creating the huge government bureaucracies of America. Reacting to theological liberalism, which tended to reduce Christianity to a social gospel devoid of the message of personal salvation through Christ's sacrificial death on the cross, Fundamentalists withdrew from involvement in social programs in order to concentrate on preaching the Gospel and saving the lost.

Aside from a few heroic attempts to help drunks and derelicts at such places as Chicago's Pacific Garden Mission and Philadelphia's Sunday Breakfast Association, efforts to serve the poor and oppressed in this country were considered superfluous to what was deemed "the real mission of the church"—converting people to Jesus. The concern for the victims of social oppression and poverty was left to the government which, during the Roosevelt years of the New Deal, spun off an increasing number of social agencies to handle such problems.

In reality, the government is only doing what the church was called to but has refused to do. I thank God for the willingness of government to step in where the church is unwilling to go. I hate to think of what would have happened to the many hungry people who were fed by government programs, in the absence of concern by church people. I choose not to think of what would have happened to the mentally retarded and the physically handicapped, had not the government provided the help which the church refused to provide. I shudder when I consider what would have happened to the elderly without the agencies of the government. The government was not designed for such tasks, but it may be that God has had to use the government to do such things because He found His church unwilling.

During the years of the civil rights movement, a church in a suburban community where my college is located became very concerned about the plight of black people living in the ghettos of Philadelphia. After much debate and struggle, the church members decided that the best way they could respond to the needs of their black brothers and sisters was to mortgage their building and make those funds available for various needs in the black community.

The church went in debt for $150,000; with the funds it secured through mortgaging its property, a variety of programs were started. Day-care centers, reading clinics, thrift shops, job placement programs, and programs for the elderly came into being within a few months.

What was more amazing was the response of the media in the greater Philadelphia area. Newspapers carried full-page stories, and television stations covered the activities of this church with spots on the evening news. Two national magazines provided coverage of the story.

At first I couldn't understand why such a fuss was being made; but little by little I realized that when a church stops talking about being the servant of God and becomes the servant of God, it is news. Nobody is surprised when a church takes out a mortgage to improve its facilities or put up a new building. People expect the church to do things to aggrandize its own stature and to provide for its own people. What amazes the world is when the church is willing to sacrifice itself for the welfare of others, when it expresses love with no thought of return, and when it is willing to lose everything for the sake of the suffering peoples of the world.

A Parable for the Church

Imagine, if you can, going on a tour of an oil refinery. The tour guide shows you the places where the petroleum is broken down into various components that are made into gasoline, lubricating oil, and other products. She shows you the way the petroleum is purified and processed. Eventually you finish the tour and ask one important question, "Where is the shipping department? You didn't show me the place where you ship out what you have produced."

"There is no shipping department," the tour guide answers.

"What do you mean? There must be a shipping department; there must be some place from which you export what you produce."

"No, there isn't," the tour guide responds. "All the energy generated and produced in this refinery is used to keep the refinery going."

Unfortunately, the parable is easy to apply to the life of the church. Instead of reaching out to serve the poor and the oppressed, the church has become an institution oriented to its own survival. Most of the money and energy of the church is consumed in promoting its own programs, upholding its own membership, and constructing its own buildings. Very few of its resources ever trickle out to serve those who are the victims of outrageous social misfortune. Very little is used to bind up the wounds of those who have been harmed by evil social practices. Only a pittance is provided by Christendom to meet the needs of the poor.

When the church, instituted by God to exercise a redemptive influence on society through love, refuses to fulfill its calling, the government steps in and does what it is not designed to do. Because the government is an institution of power, created to restrain evil, it usually mishandles the social services which are thrust upon it through ecclesiastical negligence.

11
What to Do While We Wait for the Second Coming

A Christian Perspective on Civil Disobedience and Nuclear Disarmament

No consideration of the role that Christians should play in government would be complete without some discussion about whether civil disobedience is ever legitimate for a Christian. There are many Christians who categorically answer the question with a no. They claim that Romans 13 leaves no room for civil disobedience. They say that the Apostle Paul teaches us to view government leaders as ministers of God, regardless of how evil they are. They claim that if we obey them and evils result, we are not to blame, for God will judge the rulers who directed us rather than judging us. During the days of Hitler's regime, some German Christians believed it was wrong to oppose the government, in spite of its obvious immorality. Their religious duty was to "obey the higher powers." They believed that God would not hold them responsible for what the government did or ordered them to do.

I must admit that such a position has much to commend itself to our thinking. It is a neat and explicit result of a straightforward interpretation of Paul's writings to the Romans. However, over the last couple of decades, my thinking on this subject has shifted away from an interpretation of Scripture that condemns all forms of civil disobedience.

I had been asked to deliver a series of lectures for Religious Emphasis Week at a small church-related college. I had just finished giving what I thought was a thorough explanation of a Christian view of government, when a sophomoric-looking young man rose to his feet to ask a question. "Mr. Preacher," he inquired, "what ideas have you got about civil disobedience?"

The question was relevant to the times. We were in the early 1960s and the civil rights movement was in high gear. Many of its leaders were advocating civil disobedience to call attention to the oppression that black people were having to endure in some southern states. By disobeying the laws and being arrested, many blacks felt that they could demonstrate the injustice of the Jim Crow system. However, many sincere conservatives believed that civil disobedience would lead to a breakdown of law and order, and would end the social contract that makes government possible. At that time, I listed myself among the law-and-order advocates and responded to the student's question by reading to him from Romans 13.

> Everyone must submit himself to the governing authorities, for there is no authority except that which God has established. The authorities that exist have been established by God. Consequently, he who rebels against the authority is rebelling against what God has instituted, and those who do so will bring judgment on themselves (vv. 1–2).

"Does that answer your question?" I asked.

"Not really," he answered with a nasal Southern accent that left me feeling that I was dealing with a hillbilly just waiting to be demolished. People with accents or twangs in their speech cause me to feel that they are unsophisticated down-home folk who may have some crackerjack wisdom but are out of touch with the heavy stuff that is part of the intellectual exchange of the Eastern establishment. Such *a priori* assumptions can prove disastrous.

"Where was Paul when he wrote that stuff?" asked my inquisitor.

I took a deep gulp and answered with a somewhat embarrassed air, "In jail." I cleared my voice and wanted to move on, but he came back again with another question. "How did he get in jail?"

I told him it was a long story and not too relevant to present-day civil disobedience. He ignored my response and just went ahead and gave his own explanation.

"Let me tell you how Paul got there. You see, Preacher, they were having problems with race relations down there in Jerusalem. The Gentiles and the Jews weren't getting along. They had separate churches, probably because the Gentiles had a different kind of music, were loud, and shouted 'Amens' during the sermon. The Jews were into dignity and good music and that kind of stuff. I'm really not sure what the problem was, but they just weren't gettin' along. Some of the big preachers in the early church thought they ought to hold a conference to see whether this segregation was a good thing or a bad thing. They invited ole Paul to come to the meeting, and Paul said to himself, 'I oughta go to that meeting to show them people that Jesus don't tolerate no divisions that separate different kinds of folks and that He came to make everybody one.'

"Paul knew that talkin' usually doesn't do no good. You gotta *show* people what's right. So ole Paul, he got himself a Gentile friend and decided that the two of them would go down to Jerusalem together and show them other Apostles that Jesus puts together people who the world tries to keep apart. You can read all about it, Preacher, in the Book of Acts."

I felt the crowd slipping away from me. The young man was getting the upper hand and I didn't know how to stop him. He just went on and on.

"Jews and Gentiles didn't travel together in them days. When they went any place on a boat, they stayed in separate compartments. I think the Gentiles sat in the back of the boat; but ole Paul wouldn't have none of it. He traveled with that Gentile just like he was his own brother. They rode together all the way to Jerusalem. I don't know what you call that, Preacher, but it sounds like the first Freedom Ride to me.

"When they got down there to Jerusalem, Paul knew that the rules of the city said that Gentiles and Jews shouldn't eat together, especially in a public place. That sounds like a stupid rule to us, but them Jews were serious about that stuff. They ate in segregated restaurants and wouldn't put up with anything else. Ole Paul wasn't going to tolerate such foolishness, so he found himself a public eating place, and he and his Gentile friend sat themselves down and had a feast, right where everybody could see them. It must have upset a lot of people, but Paul didn't care 'cause he was staging the first Sit-in. You can read about it in the Book of Acts, about in chapter 21."

The crowd was giggling and I was shrinking. My questioner had a smirk on his face. "It didn't end there," he said. "After they finished, Paul decided to head up to the temple. What denomination are you, Preacher?" he asked.

"Baptist," I tersely responded.

"Well, it probably was the Baptist temple they went to. They were about halfway down the street when the people realized where they were going. Paul was going to take that Gentile man into the temple and people from the Gentile race weren't allowed in there. Now it's one thing to have a Freedom Ride, and it's another thing to have a Sit-in; but ole Paul was about to stage the first Pray-in. He was gonna take that man from the other race right into that segregated temple. That was really something. The Jews wasn't about to put up with that stuff, and they rioted. They jumped all over Paul and his friend and beat 'em to the ground. There was a regular riot going on. You can read about it in the Book of Acts. Now, Preacher, if Paul was really a man of God, what was he doing in a race riot? That's what I'd like to know."

The crowd's giggles had turned to laughter, but that down-homer wasn't finished with me yet.

"You know they would've killed ole Paul except for the police who happened to show up just in time. They took Paul into what we call 'protective custody.' When they got Paul and his Gentile friend down to the jailhouse, they decided to beat them up. You see, police don't like troublemakers no matter what they stand for. That's why they were going to beat on Paul and his friend. I guess you can say they were planning to exercise a little 'police brutality'—until they heard he was a Roman citizen. It's all there in the Book of Acts."

I knew he was moving in for the kill and there was no stopping him now. He just went on explaining, "The next day they brought ole Paul up for a hearing before the authorities and Paul broke the news to them. He said, 'You guys picked on the wrong polecat. You may not know it, but I'm a Roman citizen and I got rights. You probably thought I was one of them unregistered voters that politicians can jest ignore.'

"Well, when the authorities heard that, they were plenty scared. They tried to get ole Paul to forget the whole thing and leave town by sundown. But Paul wasn't gonna let 'em get off so easy. There was a principle at stake and he had a point to make. He said, 'No way are you gonna get by easy on this one. I'm appealing this case. I'm taking it to the Supreme Court.' Now, in them days the Supreme Court was in Rome, so Paul said, 'I'm going to Rome and let them people in Caesar's palace hand down a ruling on me and what I'm doing.' He figured that he had broken the rules of Jerusalem, but that the people up there in the Supreme Court would declare those rules stupid and unconstitutional.

"It was while he was on his way to Rome that Paul wrote a

letter to the Romans. You read part of that letter. In it he said, 'Be subject to the higher powers.' Seems funny that he should say that after all he did. If you ask me, Paul figured it was OK to break some laws if the laws made you do stuff that was against the will of God. You probably don't agree with that, Preacher. You probably don't agree with that at all."

I was dead. I knew it. He knew it, and worst of all the crowd knew it. While he had jumbled up some of the facts of the story, he knew the principle just fine.

A Possible Paradox
The real question that lies before us is how a person can resist the power of the government and still be faithful to the commandments of Scripture. It is obvious that there come times when the dictates of the ruling authorities must be opposed because to obey the commands of the state would make one unfaithful to the commands of the Lord. Peter and John faced a situation in which the rulers of Israel commanded them to refrain from preaching about Jesus (Acts 4:13-20). When they had to decide whether to obey the officials of the state or be faithful to the command to preach the Gospel, these early disciples chose to disobey the civil authorities.

> But Peter and John replied, "Judge for yourselves whether it is right in God's sight to obey you rather than God. For we cannot help speaking about what we have seen and heard" (vv. 19-20).

As strange as it may seem, I believe that it is possible to practice civil disobedience and still obey the command of Scripture to be subject to the authority of the state. This is because whenever the government gives directions to people, it always gives them two alternatives. Those two alternatives are: Do what we tell you or submit to our punishment. Down through the ages Christians have found it necessary at times to refuse to obey the government. When they disobeyed, they usually submitted to the punishment the government meted out to those who did not comply with its wishes.

In the earliest days of church history, Christians felt that bowing down before the statue of Caesar would be disobeying the First Commandment. They believed this to be an act of homage and worship to Caesar, and felt that the Scriptures commanded them to offer such worship to none other but Jehovah. Forced by conscience to disobey the command to worship Caesar, the Christians accepted the second alternative provided by the government. They submitted themselves for punishment, even when that punishment meant being thrown to the lions or slain by gladiators.

Martin Luther King faced the same dilemma during the years of the Civil Rights movement. He went into many communities to protest unjust laws that discriminated against his black brothers and sisters. In his opposition to such laws, he often found it necessary to practice civil disobedience. When he did he presented himself for arrest and in so doing was subject to government.

During the years of the Vietnam War the same question presented itself to many Christian young people. Those who were opposed to their country's involvement in the war felt that they could not in clear conscience participate as soldiers. Many of these young people also rejected any role as army medics. They believed that by taking such positions they were only releasing other military personnel to do battle with the Vietnamese.

When they were drafted, a number of young people fled across the border into Canada or went to live in Europe to escape military service. I personally feel that fleeing the country is refusal to submit to higher authorities. I would have preferred it if these young people had presented themselves to the civil authorities for arrest. In so doing they would have been subject to the government, and would at the same time have pricked the conscience of the nation. Perhaps we needed thousands of our finest young men behind bars, during the Vietnam years, because they could not in clear conscience participate in a war they believed contrary to the will of God. Such action would have caused all of us to ask a lot of questions much earlier than we did, and the sufferings of untold thousands might have been prevented.

I am not suggesting that those who were opposed to the war in Vietnam were necessarily right in what they believed. I am only endeavoring to outline the proper way for Christians to exercise opposition to a government committed to action they deem opposed to the will of God. Blind obedience to the orders of a government is not necessarily being subject to the authority of government.

Power in a Nuclear Age

We live in the most unusual time in history. In the hands of a small number of human beings lies the capacity to eradicate life from the face of this planet. The dawn of the nuclear age has awakened all of us to the threats and absurdities of power. Yet, in the face of these conditions, the church has had little to say to those who wield the instruments of destruction.

Most Christians are reluctant to believe that love is able to overcome power and instead have become champions of the effort to insure our safety by increasing our military might. Strange as it may seem, those of us who call for nuclear disarmament are viewed as spiritually suspect by many of our evangelical brothers and sisters. They assume that those who reject power as a means of dealing with our enemies, and choose instead to relate to them with love, are somehow unfaithful to the teachings of Christ.

I am well aware of the fact that America is in a precarious position in relationship to Russia; in all probability, the Russians have greater nuclear resources. According to one estimate, the Russians are able to destroy every man, woman, and child on the earth seven times over, while we have the capacity for annihilating human life only four times over. Thus, the Russians are more powerful than we are. The absurdity of such an argument does not dawn on many people; they do not see that after the capacity to destroy all human life once has been achieved, we are only talking about overkill and that it is absurd to argue over which nation has the greatest capacity for overkill. I do not believe there is any question about the fact that both the United States and the Soviet Union have the capacity to mete out undeterred destruction.

There are those in government who talk about the possibility of "winning" a nuclear war. They talk about "acceptable levels" of deaths, pointing out that it is possible to wage a nuclear war in which "only" one hundred million Americans lose their lives. Such "optimistic" projections of survival from a nuclear holocaust do not take into consideration the warnings of some of the most outstanding spokespersons of the medical profession who tell us that for those who survive a nuclear war, life would be unbearable. Large proportions of the population would suffer from nuclear radiation that would cause them to vomit to death, while others would have cancer growing in their bodies at a fantastically high speed. Still others would suffer such emotional and psychological shock that normative life would be impossible.

Nevertheless, those who strategize nuclear warfare claim that such people can be called "winners." Hopefully, say these planners of World War III, the destruction wrought among the Russians would be so much greater that we could be deemed the victors. Talk like this makes us aware of the absurdities of power and the callousness it creates among those who possess it.

In light of the horrendous prospects of nuclear war, many

respected evangelical leaders have become nuclear pacifists. Billy Graham has been quoted as saying, "The present arms race is a terrifying thing, and it is almost impossible to overestimate its potential for disaster. . . . Is nuclear holocaust inevitable if the arms race is not stopped? Frankly, the answer is almost certainly yes."

John Stott, Rector Emeritus of All Souls Church in London, has said, "I cannot see any conceivable moral justification for using weapons of indiscriminate mass destruction which would kill millions of noncombatants, and I have therefore declared myself a nuclear pacifist."

Other leading evangelicals such as Ted Engstrom, the Executive Director of World Vision International, Vernon Grounds, President Emeritus of the Conservative Baptist Theological Seminary, and John Bernbaum, Director of the American Studies program of the Christian College Coalition, have called for a conference on The Church and Peacemaking in the Nuclear Age. For the first time in many years, peacemaking is no longer the sole prerogative of people who can easily be ignored as left-wingers or pinkos. Leaders of the evangelical mainstream have stood up and allowed themselves to be counted among those who believe that the military power of the dominant nations has reached such incredible dimensions that it requires opposition from all who are concerned about life on this planet.

Most people who have joined in the cause to stop nuclear war have called for a bilateral nuclear freeze. That means that both the United States and Russia would be called upon to maintain their respective nuclear arsenals at their present levels. It is hoped that this would lead to negotiations through which both sides could begin to dismantle their nuclear arms on the basis of parity. Such a process should not require either side to take unnecessary risks.

Others argue that a bilateral freeze is not enough. They contend that the time has come for Christians to take the kinds of risks that Jesus set forth in the Sermon on the Mount. They say that the time has come to love our enemies and to return good for evil. In response to those who claim that such a policy between nations in a nuclear age is not practical and will not work, these advocates of love and peace claim that we are not supposed to ask whether the principles of Jesus are practical or will work; our obligation is to live them out. They argue that we are not called to be successful; we are only called to be faithful.

These Christians who believe that radical love is the only answer to the threats of powerful nations in a nuclear age are by no means naive. They are fully cognizant of the risks involved and recognize that the refusal to threaten the communists with nuclear weapons may lead them to perceive the western and nonaligned nations as vulnerable for a worldwide military takeover. They have no illusions about the totalitarian tendencies evident in the ruling elite of the USSR. Having witnessed the tyranny of the communists in Afghanistan and Poland, they recognize that the tanks of the enemy show no respect for human life, rolling with unmerciful ease over the bodies of all who would resist the conquering designs of the oppressors.

Nevertheless, these peacemakers claim that the only response to power is love and the only reasonable way of overcoming the evil totalitarianism is with good. They say they will not be participants in a process that will destroy millions upon millions of innocent noncombatants on the other side of the globe, even if such a decision leads to the risk of being brought within the Soviet sphere of influence. They argue that the church has always done well in times of persecution and that such oppression usually leads to the purification of the body of Christ, rendering it a more fit instrument to serve God in history. Whether these people are right or wrong is hard to say, but one thing is certain—in the threat of a nuclear holocaust, such arguments no longer seem outlandish and ridiculous.

Just War Theory

It used to be that theologians and philosophers built a strong case for what has been called the Just War Theory. According to those who held to this theory, there were certain conditions under which a Christian might go to war and be justified in so doing. In Everett L. Long's significant book, *War and Conscience in America,* a concise statement explained the just war position. Ronald Sider and Richard Taylor have summarized and elaborated Long's presentation in their new and important book, *Nuclear Holocaust and Christian Hope.* It is worth our time and consideration to set forth the characteristics of a just war at this point in our discussion.

1. Last resort. "All other means to the morally just solution of a conflict must be exhausted before resort to arms can be regarded as legitimate." War must be the last resort, but that does not mean that an unjust solution must be accepted.
2. Just cause. "War can be just only if employed to defend a stable order or morally preferable cause against threats of destruction or the use of injustice." The goals for which one fights must be just. And the opponent must be clearly unjust, even though one recognizes moral ambiguity even in oneself.
3. Right attitudes. "War must be carried out with the right attitudes." The intention must be the restoration of justice, not retaliation. Anger and revenge have no part in just wars.
4. Prior declaration of war. "War must be explicitly declared by a legitimate authority." Individual citizens must not take up arms as self-appointed defenders of justice. A formal declaration of war must precede armed conflict so that the opponent has an opportunity to abandon unjust activity and prevent war.
5. Reasonable hope of success. "War may be conducted only by military means that promise a reasonable attainment of the moral and political objectives being sought." If there is not a reasonable chance of success, then it is wrong to fight, no matter how just one's cause. Nor does this simply mean that one must think one can win. There must be a reasonable probability that

the things for which one is fighting will not be destroyed in the process.

6. Noncombatant immunity. "The just war theory has also entailed selective immunity for certain parts of the enemy's population, particularly for noncombatants." Noncombatants are all those not directly involved in the manufacture, direction, or use of weapons. In a just war, no military action may be aimed directly at noncombatants. That is not to say that civilians may never be injured. If an army justly destroys a military target and nearby noncombatants are killed, that is an unintended side effect (called double effect) which is permissible within limits. But the principle of proportionality applies here.

7. Proportionality. Finally, the principle of proportionality specifies that there must be a reasonable expectation that the good results of the war will exceed the horrible evils involved. This principle applies both to the whole enterprise of the war and to specific tactics in the course of battle. For example, if the unintended double effect of attacking a legitimate military target involves killing a disproportionate number of noncombatants, then the action is immoral.

(© 1982 by Ronald J. Sider and Richard K. Taylor. Used by permission of InterVarsity Press, Downers Grove, Illinois 60515)

Obviously, the conditions of a just war cannot be met in a nuclear holocaust. In modern warfare, prior declaration of war is totally impossible. A basic condition for "winning" a nuclear war is to engage in a surprise attack whereby enemy rockets and bombs are put out of commission. There is no reasonable hope for success in a nuclear war because even the winners are fantastic losers. The nation and the people for whom the war is fought suffer irreparable damage. There is no way that non-combatants can be immune from the destruction of a nuclear battle. And lastly, there is no way to say that the good which would result from such a war would outweigh the horrible evils of failing to engage in battle. It is the awareness that the just war theory is not applicable to total nuclear war that has led so many evangelical Christians to become nuclear pacifists.

Pacifism

There are many Christians who are coming to believe that only total pacifism can enable us to neutralize the power of our enemies with love. Even as I write this, the motion picture *Gandhi* is being released for showings in theaters around the world. I have already seen the film and was both moved and shaken by the experience. I was moved because of the evidence that nonviolent opposition to evil and oppressive political domination can be victorious and that love toward one's enemies can turn them into friends. I was awed by the fact that the manner of Gandhi in resisting the English was such that when the English finally marched out of India they did so as friends. Until this day they maintain reverence and respect for a man they once deemed their enemy. As the film unfolded, I was moved by the wisdom, grace, and gentleness of a man who was willing to put love into action and make it into a tool for the liberation of oppressed peoples.

I was shaken by the movie because of the fact that Gandhi, who more than any one else in our century has put the principles of Jesus into action, was not a Christian. Throughout his efforts to deliver India from English rule and oppression, he adhered faithfully to the teachings of Jesus. With him there were no efforts to seek political revenge—when he was hit on one cheek he turned the other. He was by no means passive; he aggressively sought to love his enemies and he disarmed them by his willingness to submit to and endure the worst punishment they could perpetrate. His capacity to love his enemies while enduring their punishment and persecution makes him one of the foremost imitators of the lifestyle of Jesus.

Gandhi studied the New Testament with zeal and could quote from the Scriptures in a way that would put most Bible school students to shame. He once entertained the possibility of becoming a Christian, but there were several circumstances which turned him away from this decision.

He had often seen the disparity between Christ and Christians. He said, "Stoning prophets and erecting churches to their memory afterwards has been the way of the world through the ages. Today we worship Christ, but the Christ in the flesh we crucified."

Gandhi lived in South Africa during the most formative period of his life, and a few nasty incidents there did little to disabuse him of his notions of Christianity. He encountered blatant discrimination in that ostensibly Christian society, being thrown off trains, excluded from hotels and restaurants, and made to feel unwelcome even in some Christian gatherings.

Gandhi graciously omits form his autobiography one more painful experience that occurred in South Africa. The Indian community especially admired a Christian named C.F. Andrews whom they themselves nicknamed "Christ's Faithful Apostle." Having heard so much about Andrews, Gandhi sought to hear him. But when C.F. Andrews was invited to speak in a church in South Africa, Gandhi was barred from the meeting—his skin color was not white.

Commenting on Gandhi's experiences in South Africa, E. Stanley Jones concludes, "Racialism has many sins to bear, but perhaps its worst sin was the obscuring of Christ in an hour when one of the greatest souls born of a woman was making his decision" (Philip Yancey, "Gandhi and Christianity," *Christianity Today,* April 8, 1983, p. 16).

Gandhi came to believe that Christianity in its ecclesiastical form did not express the message of Jesus as set forth in the Sermon on the Mount. He saw that the church, unlike Jesus, legitimated violence in the cause of justice and approved of war if that would protect its right to preach the Gospel. Who knows what impact Christianity might have had on India if the father of that nation had embraced our faith? Can it be that a Hindu understood the teachings of Jesus on love and power better than the theologians and preachers of the church of Christ? We will have to wait until Judgment Day for the answer to that question.

Materialism

Perhaps our failure to abandon power and live by love is tied up with our materialism. We are so anxious to protect our possessions that we are willing to use all forms of force to ward off our enemies. A few years ago when I was at a conference of Mennonites, there was a discussion as to whether or not the pacifist position was still viable throughout their church. One elderly gentleman who owned a huge farm and had great wealth was very much in favor of the Mennonites abandoning their historic pacifist position and recognizing that there might be circumstances in which Christians could engage in war. Entering into the discussion was a young man who challenged the views of this wealthy elderly spokesman. When he had finished his defense of pacifism, the older man said, "It's all right for you to talk in this lofty manner, but one of these days they may come and take everything you have."

The young man responded, "This poses no problem for me. You see, Sir, when I became a Christian I gave everything I had to Jesus. If they come they can only take from me what belongs to Him and that is His problem."

The older man quickly responded by saying, "All right, so they can't take what you have because you have already given it to Jesus, but they can kill you."

The young man answered, "No, they can't. You see, Sir, I am already dead. When I became a Christian, the life that belongs to this world came to an end, and the new life that I received in Christ can never be snuffed out."

In frustration the older man said, "They may not be able to take what you have and they may not be able to kill you, but let me tell you that they can make you suffer."

Once again the young man answered, "When that day comes, I hope I will remember the words of Jesus who said, 'Blessed are they which are persecuted for righteousness' sake; for theirs is the kingdom of heaven.' You see, Sir, there is not much you can do to somebody who doesn't have anything, who is already dead, and who rejoices in persecution."

This young man knew the secret that made the early church such a dangerous threat to the society of its day. People who have such an attitude toward property and life are free from societal control. They can afford the luxury of living dangerously and with total abandon to the will of God.

Perhaps the attitude of this young man is an attitude that has come of age. Perhaps the hour is at hand for radically living out the Sermon on the Mount, for turning from power as a means of resolving international conflicts, and for being totally committed to using love as an instrument of social change. It may be that the challenge of our time is whether there arises a people who dare to make the loving of one's enemies a political philosophy. I myself am not there yet; but the more I consider it, the more I am aware that there may be no other option.

12
Resentment

The Sin of the Powerless

The way our discussion has progressed, one may be led to believe that sinfulness is a condition solely for the powerful. That is far from the truth. In reality the powerless are quite capable of being sinful, and one sin to which they are especially prone is resentfulness. Often the powerless are forced to accept things they detest from people who are over them, and they burn with resentment. When they are hurt, they often have no way of striking back, so they seethe with bitterness. When the powerless feel they are victims of forces beyond their control, they may say to themselves, "It's just not fair!"

The word *resentment* comes from two Latin words: *re* and *sentire*. *Sentire* means "to feel" and *re* means "again." Thus the full meaning of the word is "to feel over and over again" the anger, the bitterness, and the hatred that wells up in reaction to the injustices the powerless often endure at the hands of the powerful.

I know wives who resent their husbands. They feel trapped in their roles as homemakers; they feel taken for granted and used. There are times when they feel that they are reduced to servile creatures whose only responsibility is to cater to the wishes of their husbands. They resent the fact that they work hard all day and yet are often presumed to have been relaxing and taking it easy. They resent it when their husbands say, "You don't know what it is like to go out and work for a living."

They feel like replying, "You don't know what it is like to stay home and mind children, wash diapers, do laundry, scrub showers and bathtubs, pick up after you and the children, and run a taxi service for everybody in this family."

Wives feel resentment when it is assumed that they are responsible for everything that goes wrong around the house. This is epitomized in the television ad in which the husband is upset because there's a "ring around the collar." The wife breaks into tears because her detergent has not removed the dirt from her husband's shirt. The ring around the collar is seen as telltale evidence of her failure. The ad never asks the obvious question—Why didn't he wash his neck?

Today many women are gainfully employed outside the home. Studies show that when a woman has a job, her responsibilities for caring for the needs of the household are not diminished. In most cases the husband does not pitch in and help with housework, dishes, and laundry, and children do not become more willing to help their mothers. Instead, the working wife finds that she is expected to do all she did before, in spite of the fact that she puts in an eight-hour workday.

She resents it when her husband comes home, throws himself on the sofa, and shouts toward the kitchen, "I've had a tough day. When will dinner be ready?" She resents it when her children say, "How come you didn't do the wash? The clothes I was planning to wear aren't in my dresser drawers." She resents it when everyone still treats her as their servant in spite of the fact that she is putting in a full work week. The fact that her husband and children do not share the chores of maintaining the household leaves her feeling, "It just isn't fair."

I know husbands who resent their wives. Sometimes this resentment results from the fact that their wives are so much more adept at social gatherings than they are. Sociological studies indicate that women tend to have better verbal skills than men. They find it much easier to talk to strangers and to function at parties and in other social situations. When they go out with their husbands, they may become the life of the party, while the husbands stand in the background, grumbling and feeling deep resentment.

I know mothers who resent their children. They seldom verbalize this resentment, but it is there nevertheless. Perhaps they prepared themselves for a career and then suddenly, they were pregnant. Maybe they were in medical school or law school when the pregnancy occured. Perhaps they had just gotten a position for which they had worked long and hard when they found that the child was on his way.

Whatever the case, the babies born to such women interfere with carefully laid plans and vocational dreams. The women sometimes pretend they are thrilled by the pregnancy. They never let on that they are suffering from inner bitterness. They never verbalize their resentment, but it is there.

Otto Pollack, a friend of mine who is one of the most brilliant scholars in the field of family studies, has pointed out that this repressed resentment is felt and known by the children. He contends that children are experts in picking up nonverbal communication. While their mothers say all the right things and go through all the proper gestures of love and affection, the children pick up the repressed resentment. Dr. Pollack contends that much of the maladjustment among young people in today's society is the result of their being reared by mothers who resented them.

There is nothing in the socialization of modern women that prepares them for motherhood. They are educated in the same schools as men and are given the same vocational options. They are inspired with the same possibilities and taught to expect that their lives will be marked by the vocational successes which in previous generations were reserved for men. I believe that this is the way it should be, for I am firmly convinced that women should be allowed to realize their potential and exercise their gifts.

However, it should be obvious that for many of these women having children is an interruption of life as they had planned it. As a new mother, the highly cultured college graduate must sometimes temporarily give up some of her reading, going to operas and plays, and stimulating professional contacts. Such activities become occasional treats rather than her normal way of life. On the surface, many mothers gallantly accept this disruption of their plans, but inwardly they suffer from resentment. They feel that they have been forced into a role they are unable to do anything about. Resentment is often the sin of those who feel powerless to change circumstances that leave them feeling trapped and cheated.

Parents and Children

In our contemporary society there are many parents whose resentment seems justified in light of the behavior of their children. I know parents who have made fantastic sacrifices to provide the best of everything for their children—the best clothing, the best education possible, every form of recreation and entertainment, and all the emotional support that parents can give. Such provisions were made by the parents with great sacrifice, and yet the children treat what they have received as rights rather than privileges. They do not act as though their parents have done anything special for them. They go off to college, career, or marriage and live their lives with almost total indifference to their parents' need to see them or at least hear from them.

It would take so little effort to telephone now and then, to send a letter, or plan a visit home. But these children care little about the parents who did so much for them. The parents are powerless to change the situation—they can't make their children care. They say to themselves, "It doesn't seem fair after all we did for them," and they are understandably resentful. But resentment, regardless of how justified it may appear to be, is really sin.

I know children who resent their parents. One woman had a father who beat her and sexually molested her as a child. She was powerless to stop him from putting her through this painful ordeal. When she told her mother what was going on, her mother refused to believe her and punished her for lying. Until this day, resentment burns within the daughter. Day by day she "refeels" the bitterness and the hatred of her youth. So many people resent their parents for not loving them as they felt they deserved to be loved, or perhaps for not even wanting them. I wonder how many people would say something like, "My parents always loved my brother more than they loved me, and I resent them for that." Having no power to force their parents to give them the love they desperately crave, such children allow themselves to feel over and over again the hurt they experienced, and this is the sin of resentment.

Oppressed people are always prone to resentment. Whenever the powerless have to endure indignities and pain at the hands of those who have power, they feel justified in their hatred and anger. But what they feel is justified is really sin in the eyes of God.

Feminists

I am extremely sensitive to the value system of many feminists. Often their rhetoric and anger rise out of resentment that has been building among women for centuries of oppression they have endured at the hands of men who have had power over them. Some are reacting to the indignities of sexual exploitation that has left them with a sense of being dirty and worthless.

A few years ago when my son and I were in New York City on a Saturday afternoon, we walked by a motion picture theater on Times Square. The film being shown was called *Snuff*, a pornographic movie that presented everything that was vile about the ways some women have been treated by men. This particular film had an exceptionally debased climax—a naked woman was put to death by stabbing. It was said that the stabbing, rather than being acted and faked, was real. Made in Brazil, the film supposedly put on screen the sadistic murder of the woman. The film caught the horror and the agony of a woman being mercilessly stabbed to death. The advertisement on the billboard read, "Made in Brazil Where Life Is Cheap."

A group of 50 feminists had gathered outside the movie theater and were marching in a circle protesting the film. In addition to carrying placards that stated their disgust and opposition to the movie, the women were chanting, "Life is never cheap, life is never cheap, life is never cheap."

My son and I stood and watched the demonstration for several minutes, and then I said to him, "We should join them; we should be a part of this demonstration. As a matter of fact, the church of Jesus Christ should be here voicing its condemnation. Opposition to this film should not be left solely in the hands of the feminist movement." My son agreed and we joined in the picketing. After we marched for two or three minutes, one of the leaders of the protest came up to us and asked, "What are you doing here? There is no place for men in this protest. Don't you understand? You are the enemy! We despise you!"

I responded, "We are marching anyway; you do not own the exclusive right to be angry with evil." On the one hand, I was taken aback by her insolence and meanness; but on the other hand, I understood her reaction. She was experiencing resentment. She was voicing the reaction to pain that results from oppression, and was articulating the anger of women who have sensed themselves victimized by a sexist society that teaches man to view women's bodies solely as instruments of pleasure. She was reacting to a culture that has taught men to gain sexual excitement from exercising power and even from inflicting suffering on women.

Blacks

Black people often resent white people. When they do not, it is only because they have, through the grace of God, developed a very special capacity to forgive those whom they have every right to resent. For hundreds of years, relationships between blacks and whites have demonstrated myriad abuses of power. White people ripped the blacks from their homeland and brought them in chains across the sea to a land where they would be enslaved and humiliated. When after more than a century of slavery they were freed, they were still kept in a state of powerlessness. Refusing to live with people who had previously been their slaves, whites constructed a system of discrimination and oppression that diminished the dignity of blacks and crushed their spirit for yet another century. Without question they have every right to be resentful; and one cannot work in the black community without being sensitive to that resentment and feeling it on every side. It is hard to communicate to people who have been so hurt that in spite of the rational justification for such a reaction, resentment is still a sin and they need to escape it by the grace of God.

A good friend, and one of the great Christians of our time, is a man named John Perkins. This outstanding black leader has organized a variety of self-help economic programs for black people in the state of Mississippi, and he has inspired similar projects in other parts of the nation and around the world. As a black man, he understands the indignities that his brothers and sisters suffer as a result of racism. He knows of the humiliation his people endure in a society that, in spite of its democratic rhetoric, has treated black men and women as members of an inferior caste. However, John Perkins has been touched by the Holy Spirit. He has overcome his resentment and loves those whom the world would say he has every right to hate.

There is one episode in the life of John Perkins which he speaks of with feeling and eloquence and which graphically demonstrates the pain that the powerless have to endure at the hands of the powerful.

"I was about eleven years old when I got a powerful lesson in economics. It was a lesson which helped me see why poor families like mine stayed poor while the rich got richer.

"I stood on a farmer's back porch, waiting for him to come back with the money. I was bone tired, that good kind of tired that comes after a hard day's work. The kind of tired a boy earns from doing a man's worth of hauling on a hot, humid summer day in Mississippi.

"But if my body was remembering the day's work, my mind was flying ahead to what I could do with the dollar or dollar and a half that would soon be in my pocket. Would I buy a shiny new pocket knife? That would really wow the guys back home. Or what about a wallet?

"Not that I really needed these things, you see. But I *was* a few miles away from home. For kids in our town that was big stuff. Vacations were always an occasion for bragging—so much that the kids who did not go on vacations had to invent them.

"So that's how this thing got started, this custom of buying something while you were gone to prove where you had been. What you bought wasn't all that important. What mattered was what it would prove.

"The farmer came through the kitchen onto the back porch. I held out my hand expectantly. Into it fell—I could hardly believe it—just two coins! A dime and a buffalo nickel! I stared into my hand. If that farmer had knocked the wind out of me, I couldn't have been any more surprised. Or hurt. Or humiliated.

"I had been used. And I couldn't do a single thing about it. Everything in me wanted to throw that blasted money on the floor and stomp out of there.

"But I couldn't. I knew what white people said about smart niggers. I knew better than to be one of those.

"I shuffled off that back porch, head down, ashamed, degraded, violated. I didn't want anyone to know I had been exploited. I hated myself."

John Perkins had every right to be bitter and to carry that bitterness with him. But he knows that the Bible leaves no room for resentment; and through the power of the Holy Spirit, he has found a way to love those who have despitefully used him, even as Jesus said: "But I say to you, love your enemies, and pray for those who persecute you" (Matthew 5:44).

Resenting God

There is one form of resentment that Christians seldom, if ever, admit, and that is the resentment they feel toward God. They view themselves as powerless, see Him as powerful, and resent the fact the He has not used His power on their behalf.

One young woman was engaged to be married to someone who was not a Christian. Her pastor correctly advised her not to go through with the wedding because the Bible clearly teaches that Christians are not supposed to marry non-Christians. "Do not be yoked together with unbelievers. For what do righteousness and wickedness have in common? Or what fellowship can light have with darkness?" (2 Corinthians 6:14).

Her pastor said she should break the relationship and trust the Lord to bring a Christian man into her life. He assured her that God had somebody else in store for her. She did as she was told, and as she believed the Bible taught; but no Christian man has come into her life. She is now in her late 30s and there is a bitterness about her. She feels betrayed by God and believes He cannot be trusted. She never says so but you can sense it in the way she lives, acts, and talks. She resents God greatly. I can imagine that she is saying to herself, "It just isn't fair, God. You have given other women husbands; women less attractive than I are married; there are people who love You less and are less committed to You than I am, and they have husbands. Here I am alone, forsaken, and I will probably die that way. It just isn't fair!"

I know a couple who are attractive, intelligent, and prosperous. They have a lovely home and good educational backgrounds; and most of all, they have the ways and means to take care of a child. They have prayed and pleaded with the Lord to give them a child but none has come. I can imagine what they think as they look at teenage single women living in poverty settings with more children than they know how to handle. I can imagine this couple saying to God, "It just isn't fair. To women who don't even want babies, You give children that they will never love or care for, and yet You have denied us a baby. We would have made such good parents. We would have been so faithful in our responsibilities to raise a child in the ways of Scripture. It just isn't fair!"

From a rational perspective, the couple has every right to be resentful. But before the Lord, there can be no room for resentment.

There are pastors of churches who are filled with resentment. They have labored hard and long in their communities. They have prayed, they have visited, they have preached, and they have counseled. They have put endless hours into administration and have sacrificed themselves and their families for the welfare and growth of the church, but it has all been to no avail. Their churches have not grown, the spiritual results of their efforts seem meager, and their accomplishments lack noteworthiness. These pastors can look around and see other clergymen who seem less committed, less orthodox, less prayerful, and much more worldly, whose churches flourish and grow, who are revered and honored; and they are filled with resentment. They feel that God has not been fair with them. They may not say it; they may repress it behind an air of piety, but the resentment eats away within them as over and over again they feel anger toward the Almighty.

Confession

The first thing the powerless must do, as they writhe under the agony of their resentments, is to confess before God that they are wrong. They must stop justifying themselves and recognize that the Bible does not leave room for resentment. They should remember what Scripture says:

> You, my brothers, were called to be free. But do not use your freedom to indulge the sinful nature; rather, serve one another in love. The entire law is summed up in a single command: "Love your neighbor as yourself." If you keep on biting and devouring each other, watch out or you will be destroyed by each other (Galations 5:13–15).

Jesus wants to deliver us from the backbiting, bitterness, and pain of resentment. He wants to set us free from these destructive emotions, because it is obvious that resentment keeps us from enjoying life and from appreciating the blessings we do have. People who suffer from resentment lose the ability to appreciate the many beautiful things God has provided for their enjoyment.

The beginning of freedom from resentment is through confession. Thus I call on all the powerless who suffer from resentment to confess that the arguments which justify their resentments are not pleasing to God, and that the Lord expects them to admit their resentments are wrong. It is important to confess because that confession is a prerequisite to being cleansed. "If we confess our sins, He is faithful and just to forgive us our sins, and to cleanse us from all unrighteousness. If we say that we have not sinned, we make Him a liar, and His word is not in us" (1 John 1:9–10, KJV).

The good news of the Gospel is that if we confess our sins, we can be cleansed from them, including resentment. You may think there is some neat sociopsychological technique I could suggest, some therapy that has been developed through the research of social scientists, or some socially acceptable suggestions that could be set forth in the same way that Dale Carnegie sets forth rules to "win friends and influence people." But none exists. There is only one way to get rid of resentment and that is to confess it and ask Jesus to cleanse you from it. I believe that when you make this request, passionately and sincerely, the resurrected Jesus spiritually enters into your soul and removes these feelings which you yourself cannot handle.

It is simply saying, "Lord, You know these feelings that I have. You know how they are destroying me and keeping me from enjoying life. You know that I have tried to repress them and forget them, but it hasn't worked. Lord, I can't remove the resentments, so I ask You to do it. Please enter my life and purge me from this bitterness. Amen."

Forgiveness

The next thing that you must do is to forgive the one against whom you have resentment. In most cases there is no need for you to go to the person and tell him or her. This is something that must take place within you and must express itself in your attitudes toward those who have hurt you. For those of you who have resentment against God, you must prayerfully say to Him, "God, I forgive You."

I know that sounds like a blasphemous statement because in it is an assumption that God has done something wrong. On a logical level, we all know that He has not done anything wrong. Our resentments toward Him are unjustified and someday He will explain Himself to us so that we will understand why things were the way they were. But between now and then, what we know logically may not be able to help us emotionally. While we may know intellectually that we have not been wronged by God, many of us still feel emotionally that we have been. And so I make the unusual and seemingly strange request that you say, "God, I feel that You have wronged me. I forgive You, and someday when You can explain all of this to me, I will see that it was ridiculous for me to even pray this prayer. But between now and then, I want to end these feelings of hostility I have toward You. Forgive me for feeling like I have to forgive You. In Jesus' name. Amen."

It may be that once you have unburdened yourself of resentment, you will find that what you wished had happened was better having not happened. When I was in college I fell in love with a particular young woman and I was sure she would marry me. I dated her and treated her right. But, lo and behold, she married a friend of mine instead! I was so hurt and bitter and filled with resentment because I felt my friend had betrayed me, and this young woman had deceived me. In a sense they had, because the whole affair was carried on behind my back while she pretended to be engaged to me. It was unfair and unnecessary and I was very hurt.

Some years ago I spoke at a college where this woman now teaches. We had lunch together and I had the opportunity to talk with her at length. As I left the college at the end of the day, I found myself huming the doxology. All I could say after talking with her was, "Thank You, Jesus!" I wondered why I had been so desperate to have her as my wife. I realized that she wouldn't have been any fun to live with for the rest of my days. When I think of my own wife and how wonderful and interesting she is, I realize that I should have been grateful, rather than resentful, for having lost my first love.

Unfortuntately, all human experiences do not work out so

nicely. People are not always able to see how losing something was really a blessing because what took its place was much better. And furthermore, in some instances that will not even be the case. But regardless of what we can see or understand about the situations that oppress us, we who are powerless to change those situations must learn to confess the wrongness of our emotions, ask the Lord to cleanse us from this unrighteousness, and then forgive those who have caused us the pain. In so doing, we the powerless will "overcome evil with good."

13
Living Without Power
The Triumph of Love

The Christian alternative to power is love. Yet wherever I go, I meet people who are suffering from lack of love. Such persons live out their lives in quiet desperation, devoid of the quickening vitality that only love can provide. Sometimes they are bitter, but in most cases they are just dead. They walk and talk, work and play, eat and sleep—but they are dead. Without love people always die.

They die because they are unwilling to reveal their needs. They are unwilling to let anyone know how desperate they are to be helped and loved. They are afraid that such revelations will result in a loss of face; that people will no longer respect them; that they will lose the image of being self-sufficient and powerful.

I know of a lonely Christian social worker whose life is devoid of love. She is a person who has spent over 20 years of her life in serving the needs of people in an inner city settlement house. She has sacrificed wealth, having a family of her own, and the benefits of middle-class living in order to give all that she could to meet the needs of the poor who come to her for help. She has been honored as a public servant, has received plaques and citations from an array of community organizations, and been acknowledged as one of the most influential leaders of her city. Nevertheless, this woman suffers from loneliness. She complains that people admire her but do not love her.

The reason this social worker experiences an absence of love in her life was expressed by one of her co-workers: "She is willing to do anything for other people, but she won't let anybody do anything for her. She seems to be unwilling to let others know that she needs them."

Unless we show our need for others, we cannot be loved by them. Unless we allow people to give to us, we cannot have a love relationship with them. Unless we reveal that we are powerless to meet our own emotional needs and desperately want the love of others, there is no hope for us. This woman was afraid to reveal her needs for fear she might become dependent on others to supply her needs and thus lose power. Powerful people convey the impression that they do not need to depend on anyone for anything. Consequently, people do not reach out to them in love. This woman defined herself as self-sufficient, as powerful people generally do, and cut herself off from those who would love her if they felt she needed their love.

The Bible says that it is more blessed to give than it is to receive (Acts 20:35). This means that we need to allow other people the privilege of giving to us, so that *they* may be blessed. If we present ourselves as people who need nothing from others, we deny them the blessings which they would receive by giving themselves and what they have to us.

Recently, a missionary told me that he was not returning to the mission field because he did not have the necessary financial support to sustain his work. He told me that he was quite willing to give everything he had to the people he served on the mission field, but he had a difficult time asking for support from church people here in the United States. He explained that he just could not bring himself to let people know of his needs. He was afraid of being beholden to anyone.

The missionary thought I would laud him for his attitude toward money. Instead, I had to tell him that he had been seduced by power. "You see," I explained, "by being the giver you exercise power over the receivers. However, you yourself are unwilling to be a receiver from the hands of others because you know that this will require a humility which people who crave power do not have. You are afraid to appear in need because you think it will make you appear powerless."

What this missionary failed to grasp was this: It is not only more blessed to give than to receive—it is easier too. Receiving requires humility. It requires a revealing of need. It requires an acknowledgment that the person is powerless to help himself. Consequently, the powerful shy away from receiving. Giving is their thing.

Those of us who love power will give help to anyone who asks for it. Giving helps makes us feel good, in control, and that the people we have helped are obligated to us. We will help almost anyone, and often without asking enough questions. There have been countless rip-offs by instigators of pseudo charities, who have exploited people's desire to give. There was a case of a young man who simply stood on a street corner with an unmarked can in his hand. For a week people who passed him put over $20 a day into that can. It does not take much to get people to give, because giving does not threaten the power status of the giver. Receiving is another thing.

Who Is Neighbor to You?

One of the most familiar parables of Jesus is one of the least understood. It is the story of the Good Samaritan. Jesus told this story in response to a question raised by a young lawyer who wanted to know how to gain eternal life. Jesus reminded him that eternal life belonged to those who loved God with their souls, their strength, and their minds, and loved their neighbors as themselves. The young man responded by asking another question, "Who is my neighbor?" To answer him, Jesus told this story:

> A man was going down from Jerusalem to Jericho, when he fell into the hands of robbers. They stripped him of his clothes, beat him and went away, leaving him half dead. A priest happened to be going down the same road, and when he saw the man, he passed by on the other side. So too, a Levite, when he came to the place and saw him, passed by on the other side.
>
> But a Samaritan, as he traveled, came where the man was; and when he saw him, he took pity on him. He went to him and bandaged his wounds, pouring on oil and wine. Then he put the man on his own donkey, took him to an inn and took care of him. The next day he took out two silver coins and gave them to the innkeeper. "Look after him," he said, "and when I return, I will reimburse you for any extra expense you may have."
>
> "Which of these three do you think was a neighbor to the man who fell into the hands of robbers?" (Luke 10:30–36)

Usually when preachers preach from this passage they make the point that our neighbor is anyone who is in need. That, as Christians, we should respond to them by giving of ourselves to meet their needs. However, this is not the point the Bible makes. Jesus was asking, "Who then was neighbor to *the man who fell into the hands of robbers?*" The answer to the question is, "The one whom the man let help him out of his desperate situation." The parable is letting us know that we express love by letting people bind up our wounds, lift us out of the gutter, and care for us. In receiving help from the Good Samaritan, the man who had fallen among robbers was expressing love for him.

Think of the times you have been in need and were desperate for help. Remember how lonely you felt? It was then that you realized how few friends you really had. It was then you realized what a friend really is. A friend is somebody that you love enough to go to when you need help. In short, you will give help to anyone; but when you yourself are in desperate need, you only ask for help from people you love.

You let a person know that you love him or her by asking for help. You honor that person because in your request you are saying, "Out of all the people I know, you are the one I will trust with the revelation of my need. You are the only one to whom I dare expose my inadequacies. You are the one I love."

It could be said that the poor man didn't have much choice about who helped him. And yet I have seen people with far more freedom of choice than he had, who have refused to take the help available from man or God. I believe this parable reflects light not only on our relationships with other people but also on the nature of our relationship with God. We love Him when we are willing to accept salvation as our gift. Our love for God is demonstrated not so much in what we do for Him, but in our willingness to allow Him to do for us what we cannot do for ourselves.

Receiving God's Love

The Apostle Peter had to learn this complex lesson when Jesus tried to wash his feet in the Upper Room.

> He got up from the meal, took off His outer clothing, and wrapped a towel around His waist. After that, He poured water into a basin and began to wash His disciples' feet, drying them with the towel that was wrapped around Him.
>
> He came to Simon Peter, who said to Him, "Lord, are You going to wash my feet?"
>
> Jesus replied, "You do not realize now what I am doing, but later you will understand."
>
> "No," said Peter, "You shall never wash my feet."

Jesus answered, "Unless I wash you, you have no part with Me."

"Then, Lord," Simon Peter replied, "not just my feet but my hands and my head as well!" (John 13:4–9)

Peter wanted to do something for Jesus but was reluctant to allow Jesus to do anything for Him. He needed to be taught that he could show love by allowing Jesus to serve him. Salvation by works means that we want to do something for God so that God will be obligated to us. But that leaves *us* in a position of power. Grace is when we love God enough to receive His precious gift and end up obligated to Him. Because the gift He provides is so awesome and wonderful that there is no way we can fulfill our obligation, we will always be indebted to our Lord.

The Need to Love

Eric Fromm, one of the leading psychoanalysts of our day, states that being loved is not as great a need as loving. He points out that the human personality is so constructed that its greatest fulfillment comes from expressing heartfelt affection for others. Every person desperately needs to love and will experience joy and ecstacy at the highest possible level when he is focusing love on another person.

When I grasped the truth of Fromm's insight, it changed my attitude toward personal relationships. Up until that time, people somewhat threatened me. I was cautious in my dealings with them and was afraid to love them for fear they might not love me in return. Once I became convinced that other people desperately wanted to love me, I gained a new freedom in interpersonal relationships. Now every time I meet someone, I know something about him that he may not know about himself. I know that he really wants to love me. That does not mean that he will not be mean to me, say nasty things, or abuse me. It simply means that beneath all his behavioral patterns there lies a lonely soul wanting to love me. When I am ill-treated, I am almost inclined to say, "Come on, stop covering up your true needs, stop pretending that you don't want to love me. What you are doing is a contradiction to your real nature."

I really believe that people want to love but have been hurt so many times that they strike out because they are afraid that I will do to them what others have done. They are convinced that I too will reject their affection and hurt them. If they hurt me first, they never have to try to love me and, hence, will never experience my rejection.

I believe that every person is an agent through whom Jesus wants to express His love to me. I am certain Christ who gave Himself for me on the cross is mystically present in every person I encounter. I believe He is trying to love me through that person, even as He expects me to love Him in that person. This is the creative power of God that "gives light to every man" (John 1:9). Sin takes place when the person refuses to allow the love of God to flow through his life into mine. When he frustrates that love and creates an alternative identity which is selfish, mean, and power-hungry, I want to say, "Reject this false self you have become; repent of it and let the love which God wants to express to me freely flow through you."

Being a Christian is living with the expectancy of experiencing the love of God in every person one encounters. Dostoevski, the famous Russian novelist, correctly suggests that the real tragedy of atheism is not that it leads men to disbelieve in God, but that it leads men to disbelieve in men. He was right. As a Christian, I believe in people. I believe in their desire to love me and to give themselves to me. For I believe that in so doing they will reach their highest levels of humanity. It is sin that keeps them from this. I live with the expectancy that in every person, I will encounter the resurrected Jesus who loves me and wants to give Himself to me through this person. The secret to being loved is to live with the awareness that the person who confronts you is an agent through whom God wants to love you. It is to expect to encounter Christ in the face of your neighbor and to receive good from even the worst of men. If someone strikes you on the one cheek, you turn the other and simply say to yourself, "You really want to love me and when you strike me you only deny who you really are." When he does you evil, you will return good because you believe that he would rather have shown you love but was too perverted by the demonic to take the chance. The good news is that those who expect to be loved will be loved. But those who expect only hurt from others will be hurt.

Living With Love

As I come to the end of this book, I would like to share with you some simple techniques that will allow you to experience the joy that comes from creating and giving love.

• The first rule is to listen. There are few things that can create love between persons like attentive listening. I am not describing the kind of halfhearted listening that characterizes so much of our daily exchanges. I mean the kind of listening where you energetically give yourself to the person who is speaking so that you hang on his every word, intensely relate to his feelings, and emphathize with everything he says. It is the kind of listening that not only hears what he says but listens to what he means. Often people mean far more than they say. It is the kind of listening that leaves the listener exhausted from self-giving yet renewed through the creative power of what he has done.

When I was a student in seminary, I pastored a small church in New Jersey. As part of my pastoral responsibility, I visited the people of my congregation. Much to my surprise I discovered that several of the women in the church were falling in love with me. Please don't get the idea that I have some exaggerated concept of my own personal attractiveness. I am well aware of the fact that I am a very average looking man. My nose is long and even in those early years of my ministry, my oncoming baldness was quite evident. I do not consider myself to be the kind of person that women find attractive. These realities made me all the more surprised when several women seemed to feel romantically attached to me.

Reflecting on this from my present position, I know what happened. The women were married to very insensitive men who came home from work, sat in the living room, watched television, called it a day, and went to bed. The wives hungered for meaningful conversation and most of all craved somebody who would listen. As a young pastor, I met that need. I would sit and give earnest attention to their every word. After an hour of intensely hanging on their every expression and looking meaningfully into their eyes, I would get a response like, "You know, I don't think I have ever felt this way with a man before." I was doing what their husbands should have done—listening with the kind of listening that creates love.

One of the things that is very evident in the Gospels is Jesus' capacity to listen. He is the greatest Teacher who ever lived, the Man who had more to say than any other man in history. Yet above all else, He gave time to the ministry of listening. He heard the sick when they told Him of their troubles; He listened to the petty gripes and squabbles of His disciples; He heard the cries of the demon-possessed with a concern that no one had ever demonstrated before. Undoubtedly, His listening was the balm of Gilead that healed their sin-sick souls. To be a Christian means that we should listen as Jesus listens and thereby create the love that humanizes.

• The second rule for creating love is simply to be concerned for the happiness of the other person. A man should wake up in the morning and ask himself, "What can I do today to make my wife a happier person?" He should then set himself to the task of doing those things. The more he does to make his wife happy, the more in love with her he will be. It's as simple as that.

Many of us think we must love people first and then, because we love them, do good things for them. In reality, the opposite is true. The more good we do for people, the more we love them. The Bible says, "Where your treasure is, there your heart will be also" (Matthew 6:21). This means that what a person invests in, he loves. If a person invests in a relationship, makes sacrifices for it, provides every consideration for the other person who is part of the relationship, he is creating love.

We often think that *when* we love somebody, we invest in the relationship. In reality, we love somebody *because* we have invested in the relationship. My wife and I often talk about the love we have for each other and how it came into existence. We have also concluded that the reason why we love each other is because over the years each of us has given so very much to the other. Love did not happen. It was created through sacrifices and self-giving on the part of both of us. The more we invest in the marriage, the more precious the relationship becomes and the deeper the love grows between us.

A friend of mine tells the delightful story of having counseled a man who was falling out of love with his wife. My friend advised this husband to think of all the ways he could make life happier for his wife and then do them. A few days later my friend received a telephone call in which the husband related the following story:

> Every day I leave for work, put in a hard day, come home dirty and sweaty, stumble in the back door, go to the refrigerator, get something to drink, and then go into the rec room and watch television until suppertime. After talking to you, I decided I would do better than that in the future. So yesterday, before I left work, I showered and shaved and put on a clean shirt. On the way home I stopped at the florist and bought a bouquet of roses. Instead of going in the back door as I usually do, I went

to the front door and rang the doorbell. My wife opened the door, took one look at me, and started to cry. When I asked her what was wrong she said, "It's been a horrible day. First little Billy broke his leg and had to have it put in a cast. I no sooner returned home from the hospital when your mother called and told me that she is coming to stay for three weeks. I tried to do the wash and the washing machine broke and there is water all over the basement floor, and now you have to come home drunk."

In most marriages, consideration is so unusual that a wife could think that her husband was drunk because he was kind.

• The third and most important rule for creating love is to recognize that Jesus is a mystical presence in the person you want to love. There are those who would limit Jesus to being present only in those who acknowledge Him as Lord and Saviour, but I will not accept that limitation. I believe that Jesus is present even in those who do not surrender to Him. I do not believe that any person is devoid of the image of God. Being in the image of God is dependent upon the mystical presence of the Lord who is waiting to be loved in every single human being.

The difference between the saved and the lost is that the lost refuse to surrender to the presence of Jesus. They fight against His will and resist His desires for the life that he has planned for them. Nevertheless, He is still with them, working for surrender, constantly inviting them to yield, pleading with them to stop the war they have declared against His plan for their lives. But even if they resist God's plan, He is still there within them, waiting to be loved and served.

Those who can recognize the presence of Jesus in the people they meet will find it easy to love them, in spite of their short-comings, weaknesses, and frailties. Beneath the nasty behavior, meanness, and cruelty, they still can see Jesus mystically incarnated in those who refuse Him.

The best way I can explain what I mean when I say that

"Christ is a living presence dwelling in the person who confronts us in need" is to relate a traumatic experience that was responsible for molding my theology. I was on the Island of Hispanola, near the Haitian border. I was standing at the edge of a grass landing strip waiting for a small airplane to pick me up and take me back to the capital city. As I searched the skies looking for the airplane, a woman came toward me. In her arms she was holding a baby with its stomach swelled four or five times the normal size. This happens when children are experiencing malnutrition and serious cases of worms. The arms and legs of the child were skin and bones, and hung limply from the body. It was a black child, but its hair had turned rust-colored, also a sign of advanced malnutrition. The child was one of the most sickening and upsetting cases that I have ever seen.

The mother held her child up to me and began to beg for me to take him to the United States. Her hope was that I would cure her child and raise him as my own.

I tried to get away from her, but she would not let me go. In a most pathetic manner she begged, "Please, Mister, take my baby. Don't let my baby die. Don't let my baby die, Mister. Take my baby. Take my baby!" She kept pleading with me over and over again, and I kept trying to get away from her. I didn't know what to do. There were hundreds of babies, within five miles of where I was standing, with problems so immense that I was confused and upset. But she kept on begging me, "Save my baby. Don't let my baby die, don't let my baby die."

Finally the small airplane I had been waiting for came into sight. As soon as it touched the edge of the landing strip, I ran across the field to meet it. She came running after me screaming at the top of her lungs, "Don't let my baby die. Don't let my baby die." I climbed into the plane and closed the plexiglass door. The engine began to rev up, but before the plane began rolling, she had caught up to it. Holding her baby in one hand, she banged on the fuselage with the other. The roar of the engine drowned out her voice, but I could see her lips moving, as she still screamed at me to take her baby. Then the airplane pulled away from her, down the landing strip, and into the air. As we circled the field, I saw her standing alone on the grassy landing strip.

It wasn't long before I realized who I had left behind., It wasn't just a dying Haitian child. I knew that I had left Jesus. I fear that one day the Lord will say, "I was hungry and you didn't feed Me, naked and you didn't clothe Me, sick and you didn't care for Me, a stranger and you didn't take Me in." And I will said, "Lord, when did I see you hungry and not feed You? Naked and not clothe You? Sick and not minister to You? A stranger and not take You in? And He will say, "When you failed to do it to that baby, you failed to do it to Me."

Since that time, I have become intensely aware that every person must be treated as Jesus. Each human being, no matter how hungry or how nasty, is a vehicle through whom I can love my resurrected Lord.

The Fat Lady

In J.D. Salinger's book *Franny and Zooey,* there is a brilliant passage that communicates to the reader the way God can be encountered. In the story, Franny comes home from college psychologically messed up because of her involvement in a strange religious cult. Her beliefs are confused, her perception of reality is distorted, and her ability to relate to people is gone. Throughout the story, her brother Zooey is trying to bring her back to health and to a proper relationship with Jesus.

Toward the end of the book he reminds Franny of the time when the members of their family had a radio show, and how in preparation for the broadcast their older brother, Seymour, would always tell them to shine their shoes, straighten their clothes, and do their very best for "the fat lady." Zooey asks Franny what came to her mind when Seymour said that. He explains that in his own mind he saw a picture of a fat lady sitting on a porch, swatting flies, with her radio going full blast from morning until night. He saw her sitting there in the terrible heat of a summer day, suffering from cancer. Whenever he pictured her he wanted to do his very best on the radio show, because he was doing it for that lady. He hoped that if he was good enough, she would forget the pain and agony of her situation and lose herself in the excitement of the program.

Franny explains that she also had that kind of image. While she didn't see the fat lady on a porch, she did imagine her as having thick legs that were very veiny and, like Zooey's fat lady, hers was suffering from cancer too. Franny goes on to explain that she also wanted to be her very best to help the fat lady forget her pain.

Then Zooey drives home his point by saying, "And don't you know who that fat lady really is?. . . Ah, buddy. Ah, buddy. It's Christ Himself. Christ Himself, buddy."

As I read that passage, written by an author who is by no means on the evangelical speakers' circuit, I realized that he had grasped something profound—the fact that God is a mystical presence waiting to be encountered in every person. He is in the fat lady, in the skinny man, in the oppressed black, in a difficult neighbor, in the male chauvinist, and in the downtrodden victim of the social system. In every one of them and in every other person that I meet—my son, my daughter, my wife, my colleagues, and my friends—Jesus waits to be encountered. It becomes easy to love someone when you realize that he is not simply what meets the eye. In a mystical way, each person incarnates the Jesus who loved us and gave Himself for us. No wonder the Apostle Paul instructed us to see each other no longer only in the flesh, but to view each other in the spirit.

The Duck Lady

A friend of mine told me about a woman who lived in Philadelphia who was commonly referred to as the Duck Lady. She was given that name because she had an extreme nervous disorder that resulted in her making a quacking sound almost constantly. Once an attempt had been made to institutionalize her, but eventually she was turned loose on the streets. She wandered among the crowds in the heart of the city for several years, quacking in her uncontrolled fashion. Scorned and laughed at, she became a dirty and pathetic sight and people did their best to avoid her.

One day my friend was on the street corner waiting for the traffic light to change when the Duck Lady came up and stood beside her. She quacked wildly and at first my friend looked for the fastest route of escape. Then suddenly she stopped and realized that Jesus was there, waiting to be loved in that unattractive and disoriented woman. My friend turned to her and asked, "How are you feeling today? I see you often and I worry about you. Is there any way I can help?"

Surprisingly, the woman suddenly stopped her quacking, turned to my friend and said, "I'm not feeling well and it is so very thoughtful of you to think of me in my suffering. God bless you for being so kind."

The light changed and people began to move across the street. The Duck Lady continued on her way, loudly quacking once again. But for a moment, love had broken through. Redemptive love had at least temporarily rescued the Duck Lady from her maladies and given her a respite of peace.

Everyone becomes loveable when we become aware of the presence of Jesus in them. Every person radiates infinite value when we realize that the resurrected Jesus is miraculously revealed through them. Loving other people can never be an act of condescension when we recognize that the majestic Saviour waits to be loved in and through each of them. Serving other people can never be a patronizing act when we realize that in serving others we are serving the King of Glory.

I do a bit of marriage counseling and every once in a while I talk to a married person who no longer loves his or her mate. Often such a person says to me, "You either love somebody or you don't. You can't make yourself love somebody. You can't make love happen."

Such a person is usually trying to escape the guilt associated with rejecting the marital partner to whom he has sworn love and faithfulness "till death do us part." He is trying to evade responsibility for the disintegrating relationship by claiming that it is not his fault and that the death of love just happened. He wants to communicate as earnestly as he knows how that he would make himself love his mate if he could, but he is convinced he cannot.

I have never been too sympathetic to the pleas of such people, for I am convinced that people can make themselves love. Jesus commanded us to love and in so doing, let us know that love was a matter of the will. He taught what our most advanced insights into human personality only confirm—that love can be created by people who make a commitment to listen to each other, to care for each other, and to recognize in each other the presence of the eternal God.

I believe that love is greater than power. Only love redeems and makes us good.